NATURAL
LEATHER
TANNING

NATURAL LEATHER TANNING

Tanning with Fats & Smoke

◆◆◆

Chemical-Free Tanning

◆◆◆

Preservation & Storage

◆◆◆

Salting, Freezing & Drying

◆◆◆

Plus 6 Step-by-Step Leather Projects

MARKUS KLEK

SCHIFFER
CRAFT

4880 Lower Valley Road • Atglen, PA 19310

Photo credits: Alaka Harkort: pp. 46 top, 57 bottom; Jürg Hassler: pp. 23, 41, 42, 54, 70, 71 bottom,
76 right; Heidi Schwarz: pp. 57 top, 71 top; Katharina Ußling: pp. 10, 12, 19, 22, 26, 52, 56 bottom,
64, 74, 78, 82, 90, 100, 106; iStock.com/robybenzi: p. 28 top; iStock.com/SeventhDayPhotography:
p. 29 top 90-1 (117) INV 09832600, National Anthropological Archives, Smithsonian Institution: p. 13.

Type set in MetaPro

ISBN: 978-0-7643-6611-6
Printed in China

Published by Schiffer Publishing, Ltd.
4880 Lower Valley Road
Atglen, PA 19310
Phone: (610) 593-1777; Fax: (610) 593-2002
Email: Info@schifferbooks.com
Web: www.schifferbooks.com

For our complete selection of fine books on this and related subjects, please visit our website at www.
schifferbooks.com. You may also write for a free catalog.

Schiffer Publishing's titles are available at special discounts for bulk purchases for sales promotions or
premiums. Special editions, including personalized covers, corporate imprints, and excerpts, can be
created in large quantities for special needs. For more information, contact the publisher.

We are always looking for people to write books on new and related subjects. If you have an idea for
a book, please contact us at proposals@schifferbooks.com.

CONTENTS

FOREWORD

In 2003, Markus Klek contacted the Museum of Nature und Man in the city of Freiburg, formerly the Adelhauser Museum, where I still work as an ethnologist, to introduce me to his project *Traditional Brain Tanning of the North American Indians*.

His profound knowledge of the traditional way of life of the Prairie and Plains Indians, but especially his practical knowledge of their leather- and fur-processing techniques, fascinated me, especially since he had learned them during his nine-year stay in the USA. I became curious and invited Markus Klek to our museum to meet him personally.

At our first meeting, I was thrilled by his idea to host workshops and demonstrations on this topic, since it tied in perfectly with our then-extensive North America exhibit.

The processing of fur for protection against the weather and cold is one of the most elementary skills that ensured the survival of man for thousands of years. The technique of tanning by means of fats and smoke was known not just in North America, but in many parts of the world. Our own ancestors probably also prepared their hides in this way during the Stone Age—an ancient process in which the leather is processed entirely by hand and without the use of chemicals.

Markus Klek convinced me at that time not only with his expert knowledge, but also his rich collection of self-made leather objects, clothing, and replicas of other historical objects, which left no doubt about the high quality of his craftsmanship, which requires not only many years of practical experience, but also explicit knowledge of historical Native American and prehistoric craft techniques.

I engaged Markus Klek for a weekend workshop in which the participants were introduced to the traditional tanning techniques and learned all the work steps as well as the production and use of various bone and metal tools necessary for this. It was a great success, and the course was received with enthusiasm. There was great demand for further events of this kind, and Mr. Klek still carries out happenings and events in our museum.

His new, greatly expanded book represents an important contribution to ensuring that this ancient craft is not forgotten. At the same time, it provides a convincing and practical approach to the sustainable use of natural resources through its environmentally sound approach.

Freiburg, Spring 2019

Heike Gerlach, MA, ethnologist and museologist at the Museum of Nature und Man in Freiburg.

THE AUTHOR

Markus Klek, born in 1969 in Freiburg im Breisgau, Germany, lived for nine years in the USA, where he first began to study traditional Native American brain tanning. Today, he runs his own microtannery in the Black Forest and shares his knowledge of indigenous and prehistoric tanning techniques in courses as well as at museums and other events. He has already published two books on tanning in his own publishing house.

You can visit his homepage at
www.palaeotechnik.eu

TANNING

DEFINITION

The German word *Gerben,* or tanning, probably has its origins in the Middle German *gerwen* (Old High German *garawen*) and originally meant "finish" or "make ready." Even today, the technical term *Garmachen* is used in the leather craft. Since Old High German times, however, the term *gerwen* has been used only to describe leather production (*Wahrig Dictionary of Origins*).

The aim of tanning is to prevent the proteins in animal skin from rotting, to preserve it, and thus to make it permanently durable and suitable for human use.

HISTORY AND BACKGROUND

The processing of raw materials of animal origin is one of the oldest cultural techniques used by humans. In addition to the meat, antlers, horns, and other body parts from prey animals, hides and furs were also used by prehistoric man. These skins, however, required at least rudimentary treatment to prevent them from decaying and make them suitable for further processing.

Prehistoric man, *Homo erectus,* began to colonize temperate and cold zones of Eurasia from Africa over 800,000 years ago. It would have been necessary to refine treatment methods to ensure survival in harsher climates with the aid of warm clothing and possibly tentlike shelters.

The simplest and most original procedure was certainly to remove fat and meat residues from the skins and make them flexible by fulling and stretching—or even by chewing. These methods are still used to some extent in the circumpolar regions of the world; for example, by the Inuit. It is therefore conceivable that during the last ice age, the people of Europe also prepared their skins in this way.

However, if milder and more-humid weather conditions prevail, it becomes neces-

sary to develop other methods to produce products that can withstand wet conditions, which is not the case with mechanically processed skins. The development of different tanning processes was adapted to the climatic conditions of a corresponding population group and, of course, to their general level of cultural development and the available natural resources.

Another development in the preparation of animal skins in this context is the use of animal fats and oils, such as brain or bone marrow, in combination with smoke. For this there exists the umbrella term "fat tanning." In general, however, the method described in this book is known by its English name "brain tanning." It represents an ancient technique that has survived until modern times. It is a rudimentary but efficient procedure that does not require extensive technical equipment and that leads to a finished product in a short time. It was an ideal process for nomadic bands of hunter-gatherers.

Other tanning methods, such as pure vegetable tanning, are developments historically associated with the settling of nomadic populations and progressive craft specialization, since this method requires, among other things, large quantities of certain plant parts, the construction of tanning pits, and a prolonged stay in one place (see "Tanning Methods—an Overview," starting on p. 17).

From an archeological point of view, it has been possible to draw conclusions about the production of leather and fur clothing on the basis of analyses of tools such as stone scrapers and others made of bone,

antler, and ivory, at least since the Upper Paleolithic, which began more than 40,000 years ago, which makes it possible to conclude with certainty that leather and fur clothing were produced. Since organic materials generally do not preserve well in the soil, finds are very meager as far as leather and fur are concerned. Probably the oldest and best-known archeological leather find in Europe is the clothing and equipment worn and carried by "Ötzi," the approximately 5,300-year-old ice mummy discovered in the Alps. Various scientific studies of his preserved leathers and skins indicate fat tanning followed by smoking.

Of course, almost no concrete steps in the

A Winnebago woman tanning a deerskin. The manner in which the skin is attached to the rack is interesting. (Also see "Tanning Pelts," p. 83.)

Racked animal skins in Cameroon. An historical postcard from the author's collection.

tanning process have been handed down from prehistoric times, and the preparation of animal skins thus falls into an area that is difficult to reconstruct, at least archeologically. Here, the ethnographic comparison with populations that lived or still live under approximately similar circumstances is of importance. These include, for example, certain peoples of Africa, the Sami in Scandinavia, and various peoples of Asia. Our current knowledge about the original tanning methods comes from them. In the first place, however, the Native Americans of North America are to be mentioned in this respect, because on that continent, in particular, brain tanning was used in all cultural areas and climatic zones, with the exception of the Arctic. Moreover, the process is well documented historically and has even survived to the present day. Until the end of the 19th

century, a large part of the native peoples of North America made their living mainly by hunting. Traditionally, tanned furs and leather played an important role in these societies. In addition to production for their own needs, for centuries these peoples maintained a flourishing fur and leather trade with the colonial powers and later the USA. So it was not only trappers, pioneers, and rangers who used Indian leather. European high society also liked to dress in brain-tanned articles, at least until the chemical tannery appeared and the supply of North American hides almost ran out because animals such as bison, deer, and antelope had been hunted almost to extinction.

By the middle of the 20th century, the old tanning methods had been almost completely forgotten by Native Americans. In

Brain-tanned leather's airy, fibrous structure is responsible for its special softness and breathability.

1973, for example, there were only about ten women among 12,000 Native Americans on the Lakota Pine Ridge Reservation in the USA who had preserved the traditional knowledge (Belitz 1973). The situation was somewhat better in Canada and Alaska, where hunting and trapping continued to play an important role.

The process has become accessible to a wider audience thanks to the enthusiasm of a number of "white" Americans, such as Buck Slim Schaefer and Jim Riggs, who wrote a practical guide to brain tanning as early as 1973.

Especially in the USA, there are now an increasing number of excellent tanners, many of whom pass on their knowledge by offering courses and seminars. In addition, sufficient English-language literature has appeared on this subject (see "Further Reading," p. 134).

Brain tanning, with its long tradition, still provides a wonderful material, which on the one hand is soft like velvet and at the same time robust and durable as well as breathable. The production of durable and supple leather is therefore not witchcraft. It also requires no great financial or technical outlay, let alone toxic chemicals.

Moreover, when it comes to the motto "Clothing—our second skin," the proverbial first place goes to leather, because this material is structurally most similar to our own skin and is thus ideal clothing material for humans. If the Institute of Building Biology and Ecology in Neubeuern is to be believed, only protein fibers should be worn directly on the skin (Lehmann 1984, p. 8). These include wool, silk, and leather. Brain tanning produces a material that is ideal in this respect.

However, as far as industrial leather production is concerned, since the triumph of the chemical industry, countless different methods for the preparation and post-treatment of leather and furs have emerged. The processes are, like all other modern production processes, largely mechanized and are usually carried out with the help of various chemicals. The result is a wide variety of different types of leather that often no longer have anything to do with a healthful and natural product. In central Europe, high labor costs as well as ever-stricter environmental regulations led to the decline of the domestic tanning industry in the last century. A large proportion of all leather and hides are now produced abroad. A few large companies remain in German-speaking countries, such as Südleder GmbH in Rehau, Germany, as well as a manageable number of small- to medium-sized concerns. The last tanning school in Reutlingen, Germany, closed its doors a few years ago.

Leathers and furs processed using historical methods and the knowledge about their production are also interesting for another reason, since they provide authentic source material for the reconstruction of historical and prehistoric objects made of animal skin. After all, these leathers differ in some ways (e.g., external appearance, strength, durability, feel, wear properties, and odor) from their modern, commercially available counterparts and therefore play a crucial role in the authenticity of the fabricated pieces. Such leathers can, however, be of value not only for historical displays and reenactments in museums, but for ethnologists, archeologists, and restorers too, to whom practical knowledge of historical tanning processes is likely to be of interest to enable them to react with the appropriate knowledge to the respective challenges of their scientific fields in relation to leather, an important covering material.

I myself started my tanning career in Canada. There I tanned my first deerskin at the Northern Lights Primitive Skills Gathering in 1995. During the next nine years that I spent in the USA, I made the acquaintance of many excellent tanners, such as Matt Richards, Steven Edholm and Tamara Wilder, Lynx and Digger, and Jim Miller, as well as Dave Bethke. With most of them, I spent days or weeks learning the practice of brain tanning.

TANNING METHODS — AN OVERVIEW

Nowadays, there is a wide range of different tanning methods, providing a large number of different products for modern use, from flame-resistant leather upholstery for luxury limousines to so-called medical sheepskin for baby carriages.

In principle, however, the various processes can be grouped into three categories, although there is some overlap.

TANNING WITH FATS / CHAMOIS TANNING

As described in the last chapter, the use of fats is probably the oldest approach to making skins supple. However, experts distinguish between two different methods. First there is "true tanning," in which a chemical change in the structure of the hide takes place with the help of oxidative oils and fats. This is achieved mainly with fish oils, such as cod oil, and is known as chamois tanning. Second, there is so-called "nongenuine" tanning, which means that the skin structure is not chemically and permanently affected, and the suppleness is reversible. This also includes brain tanning. However, this is true only up to the point where the smoking is added, because after that, this method is also irreversible. What exact chemical processes the smoke causes in the skin are not fully understood, but it is known that various aldehydes are at work here. These are known from so-called aldehyde tanning and thus provide an indication of the effect of smoking. Incidentally, another method falls under the category of "false tanning"; namely, that involving the use of alum (see p. 19).

Fat-tanned hides are soft and supple, similar to what is commonly known as suede, and are often made into clothing.

VEGETABLE TANNING

The origins of this method also go far back into the past. So-called vegetable tanning has been known for at least 5,000 years, as findings from Egypt prove.

This method of tanning is based on tannins, which are found in various parts of plants and tannins from the bark of trees, principally oak and spruce. Nowadays, more exotic plants are also used, such as tare from South America or acacia bark (mimosa). For some years now, rhubarb root has also been used. Historically, vegetable tanning is known in this country as bark or pit tanning. It was mainly applied to cattle hides and resulted in a heavy, strong, and stable leather as required for saddlery, harnesses, shoes, drive belts, and the like. This was the predominant tanning method in Europe until the early 20th century.

MINERAL/CHEMICAL TANNING

Another historically evolved method, which utilizes the properties of inorganic materials, is mineral tanning. This mainly involves the use of the aluminum salt alum, which was originally mined naturally or extracted from earths and shales. In the meantime, however, the substance is produced synthetically. The use of alum in conjunction with other auxiliaries is also known as white tanning and, in the case of medium and small hides, results in fine, noble, and soft leathers (e.g., for the production of bags and gloves). Finally, the most recent development, which became established from the second half of the 19th century, is chemical or synthetic tanning.

In addition to increasing mechanization and industrialization of all work processes, the use of a wide variety of chemicals became more important in order to shorten the tanning time and thus make it cheaper. The most important of these is the use of chromium salts. Chrome-tanned hides

ON A SIDE NOTE! Combination of Fat and Vegetable Tanning

It is also possible to combine fat and vegetable tanning. In this type of mixed tanning, the skin is first soaked in vegetable decoctions for a few hours or days after scraping and then further treated as in ordinary fat tanning. These decoctions, boiled from spruce, oak, or willow bark, on the one hand color the hide in various shades of brown and, on the other, give it a more compact and firmer structure when treated for a longer period.

usually have a bluish color, and the majority of all hides processed worldwide today are treated with this method. It is associated with significant environmental and health impacts. Another well-known tanning method, likewise based on synthetic substances, is that with Relugan©, which is mainly used for sheepskins and is considered harmless from a health point of view.

ETHICS OF TANNING, LEGAL PRINCIPLES, AND HYGIENE

Historically, humans have had a very close material, emotional, and spiritual relationship with their four-legged relatives. However, part of this relationship involves the killing of animals for human use. The fundamental moral discussion of whether this practice still has a place in a modern society and, if so, in what form, must be revisited again and again; however, such a discussion is beyond the scope of this book.

The fact is that people who live in proximity to and depend on animals and the environment, such as so-called primitive peoples, have an attitude of reverence and respect toward animals that has been largely lost to modern man. This also includes the holistic approach of utilizing as much as possible of an animal that has been killed and not wasting anything. From an economic point of view alone, it's therefore logical to also process the hides that are produced. Nowadays, as a byproduct of slaughtering and hunting, these play a subordinate role economically. Very often, the skins of killed animals even end up in the garbage.

The tanning hobbyist who is concerned about this topic will also look for a tanning method for these hides that reflects this ethical approach, because the careful use of resources and environmental awareness and naturalness are, more than

From the skin to the ingredients, everything is natural and fully organic! This whets the appetite for more.

ever, trend-setting values. In this context, the approach described in this book is the most optimal method, since it doesn't require the use of any environmentally harmful substances. It doesn't require any machines or chemicals, but only patience, a bit of know-how and intuition, and the gifts of nature to transform animal skins into wonderfully natural products: an eco-logical-upcycling process.

In addition, you can gain insights into natural processes, experience traditional handicrafts firsthand, and feel the satis-faction of having made something from start to finish. Last but not least, it's also a way to get a little closer to the animals whose skins you hold in your hands.

Nevertheless, there are some things to consider, even for the tanning hobbyist; namely, the issues of animal law, hygiene, and waste disposal. Those who keep farm animals themselves or go hunting should be familiar with these regulations anyway. The tanning hobbyist, however, who buys fresh hides only from breeders, hunt-ers, or slaughterhouses, will, within the framework of the method described here, scarcely be affected by such regulations, because the quantities of waste and the substances used are largely harmless. As far as the disposal of wastes such as hair, skin, and scraper residues, there's hard-ly anything beyond the scope of normal household waste and compost disposal. Here in particular, the personal responsi-bility of the individual is called for. Anyone who handles larger quantities of hides at one time can contact local slaughterhous-es and knacker's yards, since the waste

Wearing rubber gloves during work is optional, but it is the safest way to protect against infec-tions and the transmission of diseases.

can be disposed of there for a small fee.

On the other hand, with respect to hygiene and the possible transmission of diseases or infections, there are a number of points that must be observed. During tanning, one is basically dealing with a decompos-ing animal biomass, which may also be contaminated with dirt and fecal residues. To avoid blood poisoning and transmission of other diseases, rubber gloves can be worn while working. This is recommended in any case if there are open wounds on the hands. However, in such a case, it's better to postpone the work until they have healed again.

In addition, it is possible that the fresh

skins are infested with parasites, which, as soon as the carcass has cooled down, begin looking for a new host. Fleas and especially ticks can migrate to the tanner and transmit dangerous diseases such as Lyme disease and TBE. So it's important to be on the lookout and transport hides only in sealed plastic bags. During and after work, one should check one's arms and clothing for these pests.

The deer louse (*Lipoptena cervi*) is another bloodsucker that primarily attacks wild animals, such as deer, and is particularly common in autumn. It can also sting humans, but transmission of disease is not certain.

The botfly (*Hypoderma diana*), which also attacks hoofed animals, is harmless to humans but can impair the quality of the skins it infests (see p. 29).

If you wish to tan fox pelts, the so-called fox tapeworm represents another potential source of danger. This parasite, in the form of eggs excreted through the intestines that remain in the fur, can be ingested through the tanner's mouth and respiratory tract and cause a serious disease. Even freezing of dead foxes or their pelts is effective only from −80°C. A mouth covering and disposable gloves are therefore recommended; furthermore, moistening the coat can prevent the small eggs from flying around. The wearing of special clothing when handling fox carcasses or their skins is also advised.

In addition, the issue of BSE (mad cow disease) should be mentioned, because this pathogen can be present in the brain mass of bovids (i.e., cattle). Since their brains haven't been available to the public since 2000, this pathogen does not pose a direct threat. At the butcher's, one can still order the brains of other animals. One can also make use of brains from game, or farm animals such as sheep or goats, because they do not pose a danger since BSE is restricted to the brain mass of bovids.

THE PRACTICE—TANNING YOUR OWN LEATHER, PELTS, AND FURS WITH FATS AND SMOKE

BASIC REQUIREMENTS

In principle, tanning can be done almost anywhere: in the basement, garage, or barn; in the garden; or sometimes even in the living room. The demand for space and necessary equipment is small, and theoretically, every household has almost all the necessary means to start work immediately with a little improvisational talent and without much preparation. After all, this is part of the appeal of this method. You don't need much to do this.

So, the basic requirement is first of all sufficient space, and the best place for tanning is undoubtedly in the open air, as long as the weather permits.

You also need access to water. If you have to get this from the tap and you are a bit budget conscious, you should expect about 10.5 to 13 gallons per skin. Also, depending on the skin, you will need a sufficiently large tub or bucket for washing, soaking, and liming. A 13-gallon rain barrel

Various substances used in tanning: Salt for preservation (*left*), wood ash or lime for pretreatment, and vinegar (*bottle*) for neutralizing limed hides.

A selection of different containers used for transport as well as for soaking and washing skins.

or similar is ideal for soaking several skins at the same time. For working with small furs, smaller containers are necessary.

All other necessary items of equipment are discussed in the respective chapters.

Of course, old clothes should be worn, because during the work, you may get wet and dirty. A water-repellent apron is also advantageous.

If you clean up properly after work, especially after removing the flesh and hair, there will be no unpleasant odors in the long term and nothing to attract vermin. If there is a bad smell while tanning, then something has gone wrong; that is, something is rotting, and that is certainly not what you want to achieve during tanning.

The time required depends, of course, on the size and type of the skins to be processed, but a free weekend should normally be enough for the novice to finish a leather, a fur, or a fox pelt.

ON A SIDE NOTE! Interrupt the Work

When time is short, a skin can be frozen at any stage of the work. This way it is preserved and you can turn to other things. In due course, thaw the skin out again and continue where you left off.

To freeze, you roll or fold the skin tightly together, pack it in a plastic bag, squeeze out all the air, tie the bag shut, and put it in the freezer.

ON A SIDE NOTE! Definitions

The terms "skin," "pelt," "fur," and "leather" are used constantly throughout this book.

In this context the term "skin" serves as an umbrella term and basically means the animal skin in its raw state; that is, untanned, with or without hair.

"Hide" refers to the skin of larger animals such as goat, deer, or bison, on which the hair remains intact, either tanned or untanned.

"Pelt" is defined as the skins of smaller animals, such as weasel, hare, fox, or raccoon.

The term "leather" is used to describe a finished tanned skin without hair.

A red deer in its natural habitat

View of the already scraped flesh side of a wild boar skin. The hairs are pulled through the skin during processing. Wild boar hides are not suitable for the tanning method described here.

THE SELECTION, PROCUREMENT, AND QUALITY OF RAW MATERIALS

In principle, the skins of all mammals can be fat-tanned.

For the production of fur or leather, the best suited in our latitudes are the hides of wild animals such as roe deer, red deer, fallow deer, mouflon, or chamois. But farm animals such as goats, sheep, and calves can also be used, of course. Large hides, such as those from cattle, horse, elk, or bison, can also be used, but they require much more work and are therefore not a project for beginners. On the other hand, a small deer skin is certainly the best project for the beginner.

There are some animal species that are not suitable or whose processing is particularly time consuming. My experiments with wild boar skins, for example, have been limited to few specimens. They are

A fox in a wintry forest

unsuitable for manual fat tanning, as described here, because the hairs extend very deep into the reticular layer and during scraping and stretching emerge by the thousands. In addition, the skin is very thick and tough.

The same is true of the badger, which because of its smaller size can certainly be tackled; however, its skin will never be as soft and supple as that of a fox, for example. Other common fur-bearing animals include marten, raccoon, rabbit/hare, beaver, nutria, and several others.

It is easier to get hold of fresh animal skins for tanning than one might generally think.

For example, in Germany alone, more than 1.2 million roe deer and 400,000 fox-

From left to right: Knife cuts on the flesh side of a scraped deerskin; scarred tissue on the grain/hair side of a previously scraped deerskin; infestation by the botfly. This deerskin exhibits many small bump-like growths that can rupture into holes during scraping.

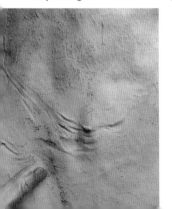  

ON A SIDE NOTE! Fish Skins

You can also tan fish skins with fat and smoke. Fish leather plays an important role in the lives of many Nordic peoples. The Nanai of Siberia are particularly well known for this. The process is basically the same as that for the skins of mammals. It is well is worth a try.

es are shot each year, and the majority of the skins from these animals end up in the garbage can!

Many hunters and foresters, however, are pleased if someone shows an interest in the skins of the animals they have killed. As a result, they can usually be had free of charge.

The only problem with this is that they are often badly damaged when they are removed from the animal and have numerous holes in them. If a fresh skin looks like a Swiss cheese, it is not worth the work, whereas two or three holes are not a problem, since they can be sewn up later.

A carcass can be skinned with minimal use of a knife without cutting much into it. Another option is to obtain skins from game farmers, who also keep their animals only for the meat and are happy to sell the skins for a small fee of a few euros.

There are also butcher shops and slaughterhouses that, in addition to farm animals, also process wild animals and, on request, may also possibly give away their skins.

Animals that have fallen victim to road traffic offer another interesting source of skins. Picking up such carcasses is officially forbidden unless you have the consent of the responsible hunting leaseholder.

Occasionally, one may be offered a skin for tanning that has already been completely scraped and then dried. These so-called rawhides can also be tanned into leather, but there is a snag, in that they have to be soaked and broken for a very long time before processing. They are therefore rather unsuitable, except for small and thin hides.

It's worth selecting all skins carefully and paying attention to any holes or knife cuts. These are cuts made during the skinning process, which sometimes go deep into the tissue and therefore weaken the skin to such an extent that it can tear at these points during subsequent processing. When buying salted hides, their storage conditions are also decisive for the quality. In addition, it is often difficult to tell how many holes or knife cuts they have, since they are often encrusted and wrinkled. Damage due to scar tissue, bite marks, or rodent infestation often becomes apparent only later, but frequently, the damage is not serious.

Once I received a deer skin from a hunter that at first sight seemed to be in good condition, except that it was covered with many small blood stains. Later, when I washed and stretched it a bit, the blood spots turned out to be small holes. It had been shot with buckshot, rendering the skin useless.

Reliable suppliers of skins that have been properly removed, preserved, and stored are worth their weight in gold, and the additional expense resulting from the special care they take should be rewarded. In 2018, five to ten euros was a common price for a fresh deerskin.

The skins of different animals differ not only in the way they were removed, but also with regard to various other factors. For example, gender and age, as well as climate and living conditions, determine the various qualities of the skin. The skin structure of male animals is generally thicker and denser than that of female animals. Likewise, the skins of older animals are firmer than those of younger animals. However, they are all suitable for brain tanning, and the choice depends mainly on what is to be done with them after tanning.

In addition, in temperate and arctic climates, all mammals undergo a molting process twice a year. This molt means a complete replacement of the coat in order to adapt to the changing temperatures. In the case of many farm animals, however, this is often far less conspicuous than on animals living in the wild. For leather production this phenomenon plays a subordinate role, since the hair is removed anyway. If, on the other hand, the skin is to be preserved with the hair, as tanned furs or pelts, it is important to note that the coat is generally longer, finer, and denser in winter. However, the inside of the individual hairs, the hair marrow, of animals such as deer, roe deer, and reindeer is very thick in winter and filled with a lot of air. This results in insulating qualities, but on the other hand, it means that the individual hairs break easily under heavy mechanical stress. Another effect of the change of seasons is that the density of the hair coat is generally inversely proportional to the thickness of the dermis. This means that the dermis is thinner in winter than in summer.

In the times of coat change, the spring and autumn, one must therefore expect that furs and pelts will lose hair. This process cannot be stopped by tanning, so skins from these seasons, so-called transitional skins, are unsuitable for tanning with retention of the coat.

As to the question of when, after the death of the animal, tanning must begin before the skin spoils, a number of factors also come into play. The further processing of a freshly skinned animal should be carried out as soon as possible, since decomposition through decay begins immediately after death. This of course has consequences that are not immediately noticeable, but the hide should undergo tanning or temporary preservation as soon as possible. Details about the methods of preservation follow below.

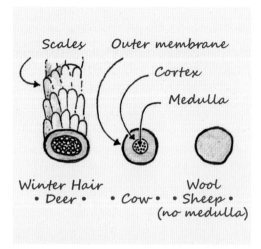

Cross-section of the hair of various animals. The hair medulla or marrow contains very little substance. Hair with a pronounced medulla therefore breaks off more quickly under heavy strain.

The prevailing temperature has a major influence on the progressive decay of a skin. This means that at moderate temperatures of around 50°F, further processing or tanning should take place no later than one to two days after the animal is killed. Cold curbs the rotting process, while warmth favors it. It is important to get to work as quickly as possible, especially if the coat is to be preserved, since the first manifestation of decay is hair loss.

On the other hand, there is a method of controlled decay used to remove hair from skins, so-called sweating (see "Liming," p. 41).

REMOVE THE SKIN YOURSELF

For those who hunt or breed their own animals, or for any other reason are confronted with having to skin an animal, the appropriate basics are described here.

The process of removing the skin is in principle independent of the size of the animal. Thus, the following descriptions can be applied for rabbits and foxes as well as for goats or deer. Each animal species naturally presents its own challenges, not only in terms of the amount of work, and the procedure must occasionally be adapted accordingly.

ON A SIDE NOTE! Alternative Cut

This is the classic cut, which is used by most people. However, it produces a skin with a narrow area under the forelegs, which reduces the usable quantity of finished leather, a problem that should not be neglected if you wish your tanned hides to undergo further processing. The remedy is to move the foreleg cuts farther out and to relocate their intersection on the centerline farther away from the chest, toward the nape of the neck. The same method can also be used on the hind legs. By positioning the cuts farther outward, once removed, the skin will have a squarer overall shape.

When removing the skin, make sure to place the leg cuts as far out as possible. This produces a squarer basic shape.

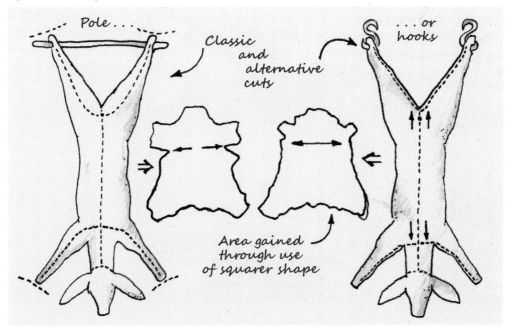

As a general rule, fresh and still-warm bodies are easier to skin than those that have already cooled down. All that is needed for this work is a sharp, medium-sized knife.

The Open Method

This is the classic approach. To do this, the animal is usually hung by the hind legs at a comfortable working height with the head down. Alternatively, the animal can also be skinned on a table or on the floor. You should, however, place a clean tarpaulin underneath and, in the case of larger animals, have a second person to help. Now make a round cut on each hind leg at the level of the heel joint (metatarsus). This is followed by a cut along the inside of each of the hind legs, meeting at the anus. A third cut follows from there along the abdomen and thorax to the throat. If, on the other hand, the head is not to be retained, another round cut follows at the neck. Two further cuts are now made from the center of the chest, each following the inside of the front legs and also ending with a circular cut at the heel joints. To make the long cuts, the blade is moved under the skin so that the cutting edge points upward, away from the animal's body, and the skin is slit open in this way in one even stroke.

This foxtail is being held open with clothespins to ensure rapid drying.

In the case of very small furs, the toes can remain in the pelt and the paw as a whole can be retained, as in the case of this marten. However, one must then pay special attention to ensure rapid and thorough drying.

To achieve the most natural and upright position of the ears on the finished fur, the cartilaginous parts of the ear are not removed and thus dry stiffly. Removal of the inner ear cartilage to the tips, on the other hand, results in "soft" but therefore drooping ears (see **"Shaman's Cap,"** p. 127).

lying tissue and pulled away toward the center of the body. In principle, the knife should be used as little as possible and only as often as necessary. It takes some practice to distinguish the different tissue forms that are now revealed and to recognize what remains attached to the skin and what does not. If you keep the skin under tension away from the carcass, in most places you will be able to get between the skin and the flesh only with the help of your fingers, a fist, or even an elbow. By applying pressure and pulling at the same time, you can usually pull the skin from the body like tightly fitting adhesive tape from its substrate. When both hind legs are free of the skin and the tail is also detached, the skin can usually be removed with a smooth and powerful pulling motion up to the shoulders. Proceed accordingly with the front legs and the neck.

Now you are ready to skin the animal. Starting at one of the hind legs, the skin is now carefully cut away from the under-

TAIL, HEAD, AND FEET

These body parts are usually skinned only with furs, and skinning poses special challenges. For example, the tails of many animals, such as deer, are small and short and are usually removed. But if it is to remain, as in the case of fox, marten, or raccoon, because it is long and bushy, special care is required. Here it's necessary to separate the hair on the underside of the tail to such an extent that a cut can be made from the base (i.e., the anus) to about the middle of the tail. Then it is a matter of carefully peeling the tail free from the trunk all the way around to this point. The skin here is very thin and vulnerable and tears easily.

However, if this is successful, a trick can be used to expose the rest of the tip of the tail. With the thumb and forefinger of the left hand, tightly clasp the exposed area in the middle of the tail, exactly where the cut ends and the fur continue to adhere to the rest of the tail. With the right hand, grasp the furless base of the tail and then, with a strong, steady jerk, pull the tip of the tail out of the remaining fur. The next step is to remove the resulting tubular residual tail skin. If the paws are also to remain on the fur, you have to be prepared for some tricky work, because it is necessary to detach the skin from each toe, if possible, to the last phalanx before the claws. When cutting the last phalanx, it can be helpful to have a pair of small, pointed pliers at hand. The thick tissue of the paws, especially on the pads, should be removed, since it dries very slowly and otherwise becomes hard and stiff.

Removing the head is another challenge, especially because of the eye and ear openings. Be particularly careful with the knife in these areas to avoid unintentionally enlarging these openings. The skin that has already been separated is best held away from the carcass, and you should always guide the knife along the skull bone from the back of the head to the ears. There you cut the cartilage at the auditory canal and work your way to the eyes. Cut through the thin membrane between the eyeball and eyelid and finally detach the lips and nose from the skull. The complete removal of the skin from predators (fox, marten, badger, etc.) is probably the most lengthy and complex kind of skinning.

THE TUBE METHOD

This procedure results in so-called "closed" or "round" pelts and furs and represents a variant of the one described above. In this process, the skin is removed without the longitudinal cut from the anus to the head and thus in the form of a tube. This procedure is mainly used for furs but can also be used on goats or sheep. To do this, the skin of the hind legs and tail is loosened and then practically turned inside out and slipped over the body like a sweater. If the front legs are to remain, these are detached separately, each with a longitudinal cut. A modified form of this method is to loosen the skin from the head. This is done by making a single incision around the mouth and rolling up the skin from there, like a sweater or a stocking, and in this way removing it from the body toward the anus. A very tricky and tedious job, but one that is rewarded with a fur that is completely intact. The legs can also remain intact or must at least be ex- posed at the ends with short longitudinal cuts. Experimentation is allowed here. As the English say: "There is more than one way to skin a cat."

Doing the skinning yourself has a number of advantages. On the one hand, you get to know the animal and its anatomy, and on the other, the pelt can be removed from the carcass in the desired way.

In the case of carcasses that have already cooled, the skin is quite tight, and

Salting and storing fresh skins in a cool room in the cellar

it requires more work to loosen it. In order to avoid holes in the fur, use of the knife should be kept to a minimum. On the other hand, when no amount of pulling helps, as for example in the case of the skin of a fat badger or a wild boar, the skin must be literally cut loose from the body.

PRESERVATION AND STORAGE OF RAW MATERIALS

If fresh skins cannot be processed immediately, they must be preserved to prevent rotting, or "stinking up the place" as the Germans put it. Otherwise, they become useless for further processing. How long a skin is considered fresh and usable depends on time and temperature factors, and also on whether or not the hair coat is to be preserved. In a warm and humid environment, damage can occur very quickly, while cooled skins can remain fresh for a few days before they need to be preserved.

There are basically three available methods of preservation: salting, freezing, and drying.

Salting
Salting is the most common method of preservation. Salted hides can either be made into leather or processed with the coat intact.

For this method you need enough salt and a suitable storage place. Road or deicing salt or feed salt for livestock can be used for large skins. The finer the grain size, the better for the skin. To preserve furs, on the other hand, it is advisable to use particularly fine-grained table salt. Salting and storage should be done in a cool, dry place. In addition, take care to ensure that liquids leaking from the skins can drain off, so that the hides do not rest in a brine; otherwise bacteria can form that may damage the skins. To salt deer, sheep or similar skins, lay them flat on the floor with the flesh side up and spread out all folds and overlapping areas. Then apply abundant salt to the raw material and spread it evenly. As a rule of thumb, the required amount of salt is equal to about 30% of the weight of the skin. For a fallow deer, 2 pounds of salt is sufficient in any case. There should always be enough salt available, and it should not be spared. Now the skin can be folded flesh side to flesh side, or you can place the next skin on top with the hair side down and proceed in the same manner until a whole stack has been formed. A wooden pallet or some similar structure makes a suitable base for this.

In this way, the skins can be stored for many months. If you want to be on the safe side, it is worthwhile salting the skins again after some time, when a large part of the liquids has already drained off.

When salting fine furs, such as fox and marten, more care should be taken, and most of the flesh should be removed beforehand (see p. 101). Sufficient salt must be applied, especially to the head and paws. Disadvantages of salting are that inadequate salting may result in damage to the skin and that before tanning, all salt must be rinsed out with plenty of water. After tanning, hides that have not been adequately desalinated often have a tendency to draw water from the atmosphere and then feel slightly clammy.

Freezing

The simplest method of preservation, however, is freezing. For small furs, the amount of space required is small. Larger quantities of pelts naturally require correspondingly more space. Freezing is simple and safe and requires little further expla-

nation. The skins or furs are tightly rolled up or folded and put into a plastic bag. All air is squeezed out of the bag, then it is knotted and put in the freezer. In this way, skins can be preserved almost indefinitely.

Drying

Finally, drying removes the moisture from the skin and thus protects it from rotting. To do this, however, the skins must first be largely free of flesh and fat residues. Large skins are then spread out flat with the entire flesh side exposed to the air. There should be no overlapping areas, so that rapid and complete drying can take place with good ventilation. However, prolonged exposure to direct sunlight with

Different methods of racking a skin for drying.

high temperatures should be avoided during drying, since this can damage the hides. For drying, the skins can be laid out flat and nailed to a wooden support, such as a wooden wall, board, or slatted frame. The flesh side faces outward, and the nails should be long enough to maintain some distance between the support and the hide to ensure adequate air circulation. Typically, 1.5-inch nails are good all-rounders for small and medium skins, and to ensure even, neat stretching, use at least 40 to 50 nails for one deer skin. Hides can also be simply hung over a tightly stretched line to dry. In this case, the flesh side again faces upward, and the line must run along the backbone. Here, it is important to occasionally smooth out any areas that curl up to ensure rapid drying, or to smooth out these areas along the edges of the skin with small sticks sharpened on both sides, so-called skewers, to keep these areas open along the edges of the skin. However, such skins will of course never dry as wrinkle- and dent-free as nailed ones. If you want to tan a skin as a fur later, it is best to stretch it in a frame and dry it there. A more detailed description of this method can be found in the chapters "Tanning Pelts" (p. 83), and "The Rack and Racking" (p. 85). Skins or especially furs that have been removed using the tube method—that is, round ones—are dried in a special way. This requires so-called tensioners. These are elongated, wedge-shaped structures made of wood, which are inserted from the underside of the fur tube in order to stretch it and keep it open. The flesh side faces to the outside. Special attention is required for the tail and paws, so that they do not curl up and rot. Clothespins may be used here to hold them up, or one can cover the flesh side with strips of paper that are pressed firmly onto the surface. Fur tensioners can be made either simply from a board or can be constructed from wooden slats. Their size must correspond to the skin to be dried. However, one can also stuff the fur tube to be dried with dry grass, newspaper, or rags and then simply hang it up. One must be particularly careful, however, to ensure that no folds and overlaps form.

The advantage of drying lies in the fact that there are no associated costs. Dried skins can also be stored for a very long time, but there is a risk of insect infestation (see p. 84).

Drying is particularly unsuitable for very large and especially thick hides, since these can hardly be soaked again before tanning, unless they are scraped thin beforehand (see "Tanning Furs," p. 99). Before leaving the skins to dry, they should be at least roughly fleshed. This means that large pieces of meat and fat adhering to the skin must be removed so that the skin can dry quickly. This work can only be done with the fingers or with the aid of a knife.

THE BASICS OF TANNING LEATHER

This chapter serves as an introduction to fat tanning or brain tanning, since this method is associated mainly with the production of leather. Therefore, this part should be read through first, since the following two chapters are based on the knowledge imparted here, and commonalities are not repeated.

WASHING

A fresh hide does not require any special washing prior to leather production. It can be sent directly to the following liming process. On the other hand, all salt must first be removed from salted hides.

Excess quantities can first be shaken off or removed from the surface with a scrubber. To do this, the skin is spread flat, and the flesh side is brushed like a carpet. Caution is advised, since salt in larger quantities has an herbicidal effect. So if you work in the garden, you must choose an appropriate place for brushing or place a tarpaulin underneath. This is followed by washing of the skin to dissolve the residual salt. To do this, it is best to work under running water in a river, stream, or well. If the skin is rinsed in a container, the water must be changed once or twice. Some salted skins are somewhat dried and must therefore remain in the water longer until they are fully flexible again.

The salt must be removed from salted hides before further processing.

LIMING

The liming agent is a strongly alkaline lye, which is used for pretreatment of the skin. This process loosens the hair and epidermis. The skin swells and is easier to scrape. In addition, the liming process leads to what is called "opening up of the skin." This means that certain fatty and protein substances in the skin, which hinder tanning, are flushed out to improve the penetration of the fats into the dense skin structure.

If you work without liming, which is also possible, because of the absence of skin, loosening the skin will have to be placed in the tanning substance (see p. 53) more often to achieve comparable results.

A simple and original variant of liming is the so-called sweat, in which the skin is pre-swollen in water for a few days and then stored in a moist environment. This is a controlled rotting. Through the work of bacteria, the hairs are loosened, which is the right time for the following step of scraping. However, this is also accompanied by a more intense development of odors, which are perceived as unpleasant by some people, but this in no way affects the smell of the finished leather. However, if the skin remains lying too long and really begins to stink, you should see to it that you get rid of it, because then it really is rotting and is no longer usable. If it's warm, the sweating process takes place more quickly; if temperatures are around the freezing point, the development of bacteria is greatly delayed or doesn't take place at all. One should therefore check the skin once or twice a day and carry out the following test: If the hair comes out in clumps when pulled gently, it is definitely time to remove the hair. However, this method results in an insufficient degree of skin loosening.

The liming agent was originally made with the help of wood ash, as the name suggests. Anyone who has access to abundant wood ash can use it. The ash from hardwoods such as beech and birch gives higher pH values and is therefore preferable. A pH value of 13 is considered ideal to obtain all the benefits of the liming process, especially skin loosening. Weaker solutions only partially remove the hindering protein substances.

Rubbing the ash mixture into the flesh side of a deerskin.

The ash should be free of coal fragments and other impurities. For this, it can be sieved. One possibility is to mix the ash with water to form a liquid slurry, with which the flesh side of the skin is thickly coated. After that, fold the skin, retaining the liquid inside. To do this, place the skin in a bucket or tub to let the lye soak in. The technical term for this in German is *Schwöde*, or the place where hides are limed.

Another possibility is to mix the ash together with plenty of water in a tub or barrel and then to immerse the skins directly in this solution. This requires larger amounts of ash, especially to achieve the appropriate pH value. Once the liming process is finished, the skins should be cleaned of ash and charcoal residues, since these can otherwise permanently stain the skins during scraping. This usually requires large quantities of water.

An ideal alternative to ash is the use of slaked lime (potassium hydroxide). Powdered lime is available cheaply in hardware

A large plastic barrel is filled with ash liquor and the skins are placed in it.

stores and is also very simple to use. Lime is non-toxic but can cause irritation when inhaled. For a so-called lime scrubber, you also need a container with a capacity of about 10 gallons, which you fill with water and then add about 2 pounds of lime and stir. This also produces a strongly alkaline solution or lye. Too much lime cannot be used, since the solution will eventually become saturated at exactly the right point for skin breakdown. Now the skin is placed in the container. Occasionally it must be weighted down with stones or the like; otherwise it will float on top and the liming solution will not reach some areas. This is especially true with winter hides from deer and roe deer, since their hairs are air-filled and therefore they float on top. The hides remain in the liming solution for several days until the hairs begin to separate. This can take four or five days, or longer, depending on temperatures and the size of the hide. This is because, as already mentioned, higher temperatures accelerate all the processes involved in treating hides, whereas a cooler climate slows them down. Once or twice a day, the skins should be moved with a stick and the liming solution stirred to ensure even wetting of the skins and to restir the lime or ash.

Strong alkaline solutions are irritating and dry the skin. It is therefore advisable to wear rubber gloves. The container should also have a lid to prevent accidents involving children or pets. In case of contact with eyes, rinse them with plenty of water.

After a few days in the liming container, the process is checked by pulling the hairs. If the hairs come out without further ado, the process is complete and the skin can be sent to the scraper. By this stage it is swollen, has a rubbery consistency, and feels somewhat slimy or soapy. This change is due to the action of the lye. Both lime and ash solutions can be used several times with no decrease in their effectiveness.

A skin that has been placed in the liming solution is tested for hair loss.

SCRAPING THE RAW MATERIAL (REMOVING THE HAIR AND FLESH)

The following scraping step serves to remove the hair as well as the epidermis and papillary layer/grain layer located underneath. On the other side of the skin, the flesh side, fat and flesh residues are removed as well as the underlying subcutaneous layer. All these operations are performed in the wet state on the tanning beam. This method is therefore known as wet scraping. Especially with very large skins, such as those of elk or bison, the so-called dry scraping method can also be used, which is not described in more detail here but corresponds to the processing of pelts and is discussed below.

THE FLESHING BEAM

For this purpose, one uses a log about 8 inches in diameter, its length corresponding approximately to the eye level of the tanner. Larger diameters increase the contact area between the skin and the scraper and therefore allow faster work, although the necessary effort is increased, which can prove to be very strenuous in the long term, especially with large and thick skins. Conversely, the same applies to correspondingly thinner cross sections.

The log should be completely debarked and have a smooth and defect-free surface at least in the main working area facing the tanner. Uneven surfaces, cracks caused by drying, or knotholes are to be avoided; otherwise the thinner parts of the hides may be damaged during scraping. In principle, any type of wood can be used for the fleshing beam. Softer types of wood yield somewhat during scraping, which reduces the risk of scraping holes in the hide. Linden is a very good choice. One should always make sure that the wood is well dried and that no resin or other sap is leaking out. Especially with tree species whose

An upright tanning beam for scraping skins

Two different types of tanning beam for scraping skins

contact with the wall and ground or floor.

As an alternative to angling the beam, it can also be split or sawn lengthwise. Ideally this results in two beams while at the same time reducing weight, which is an advantage if you plan to transport the beam frequently.

The classic fleshing beam in tanneries is a trestle mounted at waist height. Such a structure requires a different working posture. Alternatively to naturally grown complete tree trunks, logs can of course also be purchased and prepared accordingly. The use of sturdy plastic tubes with the appropriate diameter is of course also a possibility.

The skin is now placed over the beam with the flesh side facing up and is clamped between the beam and the wall. This prevents it from slipping off while being worked on.

This historical photograph shows a tanner at a classic tanning beam scraping a sheepskin. The skin is held in place by pressure exerted by his upper body. The scraper appears to be a worn-out scythe blade. Russia, 1940s. From the author's collection.

bark contains tannic acids or dyes, such as oak, spruce, willow, and alder, proper removal of the bark and bast is necessary to avoid permanent discoloration of the skins.

The fleshing beam is leaned at an angle against the side of a house, a barn door, or a similarly stable, vertical surface. This must also be clean, at least at the point of contact, and free of residues that could damage or contaminate the raw material being scraped. To give the beam a more secure stand, it's advisable to set the beam at an appropriate angle at the points of

The Scraper

An unbeatable tool for scraping the flesh and hair side is a drawplate or barking iron, such as is used for woodworking. These are easily found at specialty stores or flea markets.

The blade of the scraper, however, must not be really sharp, because the process of removing the hair and flesh is scraping and not cutting. On the other hand, the blade needs sufficient bite to remove the undesirable layers without damaging the underlying dermis. One should be able to run one's finger vigorously over the blade without injuring oneself. The Native Americans mainly used bone tools for this purpose, specifically large rib bones or specially prepared metatarsal bones.

Scraping with a bison rib. Original tools like this one work wonderfully.

Various scrapers used for tanning. *On the left,* three drawing knives; *on the right,* two scrapers for softening; *underneath,* an emery block for grinding and roughening the surface; and *between them,* a narrow-blade scraper for working on pelts.

ON A SIDE NOTE! Grain Leather

One can also leave the grain intact. This results in a leather with a smooth, waxy surface, which is less stretchy. The surface can be treated with wax grease after tanning, which increases its water-repellent properties. Processing into leather after scraping is the same, except that the grain side must be treated with special care and must not be worked on with tools during the softening process; otherwise it will be damaged. Such grain leather is smoked only from the flesh side.

Scraping the Hair Side

In addition to the removal of the hair, the scraping of the hair side also includes removal of the grain layer, which lies directly underneath. The scraping of the grain layer results in the typical velvety and grippy surface of brain-tanned leather.

Hides that have been softened or limed for too short a time are often difficult to scrape and should be resoftened. Skins soaked for too long, on the other hand, have a tendency to become damaged at holes, cuts, and thin areas during scraping, since the fiber mesh is already weakened. In addition, skins can be so slippery after liming that they repeatedly slip off the beam. If this is the case, they must first be rinsed in fresh water with the addition of a little vinegar (see "Neutralization," p. 53).

When removing the hair, work with the natural flow of the hair to the degree possible. Scraping "against the grain" can result in the hair not being scraped out, but merely cut off. This leaves hair roots in the skin, which are often visible as a blackish discoloration in the finished white leather.

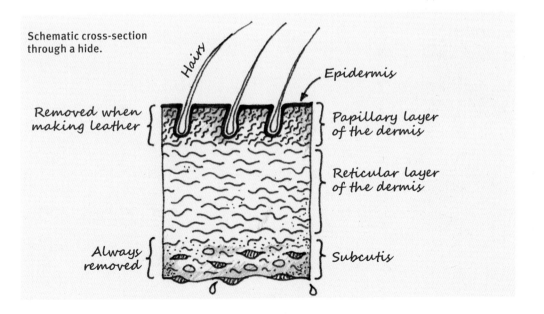

Schematic cross-section through a hide.

Hair

Epidermis

Removed when making leather — Papillary layer of the dermis

Reticular layer of the dermis

Always removed — Subcutis

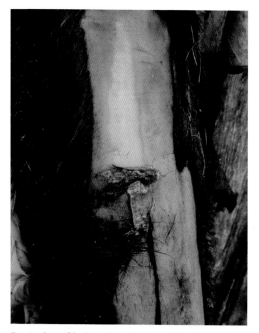

Removing of hair and grain layer. The beige layer is the dermis.

just about forgivable on white leather, but should the hide end up being smoked, these spots are extremely detrimental, since they hardly take on the color of the smoke and thus always remain visible as unsightly, light-colored spots or streaks.

Therefore, in scraping it's important to be able to recognize the grain layer as such. This also requires some practice, since it is barely distinguishable in color from the underlying reticular layer. In skins coming out of liming, it stands out better in color against the amber or beige background of the hide. Its surface is smoother and shinier than the dermis; it also appears somewhat spongier when fully soaked.

In the case of a fresh deerskin that has not been limed, on the other hand, it is often slightly pinkish in color compared to the reticular layer. Even with the same pretreatment, the grain layer can sometimes appear clearly defined and millimeters thick, whereas in another skin it again sticks to the underlying fibers like a thin postage stamp.

Therefore, for scraping, the hide is first fixed with the neck between the beam and the pad and scraped from the neck down. When removing the hair, it is important to completely scrape off the grain layer. Sufficient time should be taken to ensure that this is done. Some experience is necessary for this, and the beginner is advised to scrape too much rather than too little.

Thorough removal of the grain layer is so important because it rests on the hide like a protective layer and later impedes the complete penetration of the tanning substance, which in turn makes softening more difficult. In addition, incompletely scraped areas appear as smooth, shiny areas on the finished leather, compared to the loose reticular layer. This may be

It is therefore safest to proceed systematically here as well, and to scrape each area vigorously until no more material can be removed. The relatively blunt scraper cannot remove anything from the underlying layer, so there is no need to be afraid of going too deep and scraping holes in the skin. Moreover, thorough scraping ensures that blood residues and other watery impurities are squeezed from the skin. The tool is therefore placed on the neck and scraped with long, powerful, and even strokes. Work is done with a natural movement from top to bottom. When scraping, it is advisable to systematically place one scraper next to the other and let them overlap slightly. One should always stand straight and upright, since a cramped or stooped posture quickly leads to fatigue.

Once the entire area resting on the beam has been scraped free, the skin is repositioned slightly, and the tissue is removed from adjacent areas. This is how you process the entire skin.

Particular care is required on the flanks, at holes and cut surfaces. Here the skin is particularly thin or weakened, and holes can develop if too much pressure is applied.

Every now and then, you'll have to clean the blade of the scraper of tissue remnants; otherwise it'll merely slip over the skin and not have the necessary "bite." The skin should always be smooth and tight over the beam, without wrinkling. It must also not dry out too much during scraping; otherwise the grain layer will shrink, making it barely visible and almost indissolubly fused to the reticular layer.

The grain layer is particularly stubbornly attached to the dermis at the end of the neck and legs. The amount of work required there is disproportionate to the area to be gained, and these areas are often simply cut off. The same is true of teats, scrotums, and tails, which may still be present. However, if one is concerned with authentic reproductions of clothing worn by Native Americans, for example, one will also retain the extremities, which occasionally took on decorative and functional significance. One may even want to retain hair remnants at the extreme end of the legs, as seen on original museum pieces.

Since scraping involves some physical labor, it's worth taking the occasional break to stretch a bit; otherwise you are bound to get sore muscles.

Often during removal of the hair, the larger

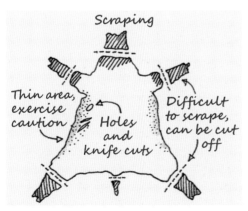

Diagram of a skin: what to consider when scraping

flesh and fat residues adhering to the flesh side interfere with clean removal of the grain layer. If this is the case, one turns the skin over, devotes oneself first to a rough removal of the flesh, and afterward returns to the scraping of the grain layer. Until the skin has been scraped, one will switch back and forth a few times in this way, because if one starts with the flesh side, on the other hand, the hairs that now lie between the beam and the skin often act like a cushion, which also makes cleaning this side more difficult.

Scraping the Flesh Side

The fleshing process involves the removal of all flesh and fat residues as well as the subcutaneous tissue.

To do this, again fix the skin with the neck between the tanning beam and the wall and start scraping as described above. First remove all coarse fat and meat residues and then proceed to the proper removal of the subcutis. Here, too, one proceeds systematically and stroke by stroke. A skin is finished when, similar to the treatment of the hair side, no more material can be removed from the same area despite vigorous scraping.

In addition, a closer look reveals branching, slightly deepened lines on the surface of the skin. These are caused by veins and are a further indicator that the skin has been sufficiently scraped at this point.

A beginner may need two hours to scrape a deer skin. However, with some experience,

this is more likely to be reduced to half an hour. Of course, the amount of time spent depends on the size of the skin. For example, just fleshing a bison hide sometimes took at least five hours. Proper removal of the subcutaneous layer is desirable, but not quite as important as scraping off the grain layer, since any residue still adhering to the finished leather will later be noticeable only as fuzzy buildups and can be sanded off.

A skin that has been limed and fully scraped, ready for tanning, is called a "flay" in tanner's parlance.

ON A SIDE NOTE! Using the Scraping Residue

In the past, all skin scrapings were recycled. Until the 20th century, the resulting hair was collected, cleaned, and used as insulating or filling material for upholstery and saddles, as well as a mortar additive or for felt production. Some tanneries even supplied the Zeppelin Works on Lake Constance with light and hollow deer hair for the interior insulation of airships. The scrapings from the meat side were also used. This so-called glue stock was used for the production of hide glue, because boiling down hide waste produces a versatile adhesive. Any scraping residue produced can also be composted, since it contains valuable nutrients for the soil, such as nitrogen. Many gardening books mention the use of hair, feathers, and blood and bone meal as compost additives.

Rawhide

A completely scraped skin at this stage can also be dried, obtaining so-called rawhide. It's quite a useful product.

Rawhide is versatile and can be used to make a wide variety of items, such as moccasin soles if it's thick enough, but also containers of all kinds or for drum coverings, as well as for straps and ropes. Such air-dried hides can be stored almost forever, to be soaked again on occasion and then processed into leather. As described above, they should be stretched in a well-ventilated and dry place.

Fleshing. Above the scraper, the clean dermis has been revealed.

ON A SIDE NOTE! Use of Rawhide

The Plains Indians, for example, made their shields from shrunken and compacted bison neck rawhide. These were known to deflect even musket balls. In carpentry shops, damp rawhide straps were used to hold glued wood pieces together, since the straps contracted as they dried. In various circumstances, rawhide was also used as a substitute for window glass and to cover lampshades. Parchment is also made from untanned, dried animal skin.

NEUTRALIZATION

If you have subjected your skin to liming, it is important to neutralize the alkaline content of the skin or to lower the pH content In the skin after liming. A pH value of 6 (i.e., a slightly acidic state) is considered ideal. If the skin has not been scraped, this process is not necessary.

Neutralization or decalcification used to be achieved by placing the skins in running water for a sufficient amount of time. If this is not possible for you, or if you are afraid that "your skins will swim away," you can also fill a bucket with water and cause neutralization by adding a little vinegar. The acidic vinegar causes an accelerated neutralization, so that you can often continue working after a few hours instead of waiting for days. For this purpose, one coffee cup of ordinary vinegar to 2.5 gallons of water is ideal. The skin is now put in and occasionally stretched a little but otherwise left to rest. The alkaline skin and the acidic water will now equalize their pH values by diffusion. It can be seen and felt that the skin gradually changes from the alkaline rubbery state with a creamy tint to its relaxed original state. Within several hours at the latest, it should feel completely limp like a wet towel or sheet. It is no longer swollen and slimy, but again thinner, grippy, stretchy, and white in color. Of course, here too the time required again depends on the size and thickness of the skin. If the skin does not seem to progress after several hours in the water or if stiff, swollen areas remain, especially on the torso, wring out the skin, empty out the water, and fill the bucket again. The use of too much vinegar can cause the skin to become too acidic and thus swell slightly. Purely optically, one then has the feeling of having done nothing at all.

Hides are best rinsed in a flowing body of water. The movement of the water promotes neutralization of the lye. But be careful to secure the skins well, so that they do not float away.

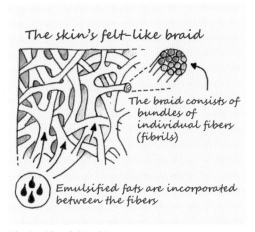

The skin's felt-like braid

The braid consists of bundles of individual fibers (fibrils)

Emulsified fats are incorporated between the fibers

The inside of the skin

PREPARATION AND APPLICATION OF THE DRESSING

After the scraping and decalcification is finished, the actual transformation of the raw skin, or pelt, into leather begins.

The first step is to produce the necessary dressing.

As the name "fat tanning" or "brain tanning" indicates, it mainly involves fats of animal origin. Various peoples used the brains of animals, meat broth, butter, eggs, fish roe, or milk for this purpose. However, the liver, various vegetable substances, and many other ingredients also appear in historical recipes. German tanners also occasionally used brains in their mixtures until the early 20th century, as handed-down recipes show. However, the purpose is always to produce an aqueous emulsion that enables the dissolved fats to be transported into the fibrous structure of the skin.

The brain of a red deer.

ON A SIDE NOTE! Why Use Brains?

Why brain, of all things, for tanning? Brain not only contains more or less "gray cells" but is also very rich in fats. These fats are what the tanner is after, because the fats in the brain, but also those in egg yolks and milk, naturally form a compound (emulsion) with water and are therefore particularly suitable for penetrating the fiber mesh of the skin. All other fats or oils require the addition of an emulsifier in order to combine with the transport medium water. Fat-dissolving surfactants, such as those found in dishwashing detergents, are well-known emulsifiers.

There, they are supposed to coat them and provide "lubrication" for them so that the individual fibers can move against each other and retain their suppleness even when dry.

Another possibility, however, is to incorporate fats directly into the hides without water as a transport medium. This is known from the old chamois-tanning process. Here, large mechanical fulling hammers are used, which knock the cod liver oil used into the hides with great force.

The use of an animal's brain tissue to tan its own hide adds another spiritual dimension in the traditional indigenous context in North America. According to research by Morgan Baillargeon of the Canadian Museum of Civilization, tanning is not only a physical transformation of fresh skin into leather, but also a spiritual transformation and revitalization. The soul and the power of the animal are transferred into the leather with the help of its brain, the seat of the soul, and thus come back to life. So if you want to use brain, you can use ones from sheep or pigs and order it from the

ON A SIDE NOTE! Quantity of Brain

There is a notion that every creature has enough brains to tan its own hide. American tanner Jim Miller, who taught me how to tan bison skins, quipped that this was true most of the time, with the exception of bison and teenagers!

ON A SIDE NOTE! How Much for a Deerskin?

The recommended mixture for a deerskin is six to eight egg yolks, 4 heaping tablespoons of finely grated curd soap, and 3 tablespoons of sunflower or olive oil.

butcher. The brains of cattle are no longer available because of the danger of BSE. In addition, you may be able to get the head of the animal from the hunter or breeder who gave you the skin. Brain extraction is generally done through the skull. To do this, first skin the head and then carefully make an incision around the entire top of the skull with an ordinary fine-toothed saw. The cut should be deep enough to cut through the bone but not damage the brain. The skull can then be lifted off and the brain removed (e.g., with a tablespoon). However, if the skull is that of a pricket, either deer or roe deer, a central

saw cut can also be made between the two antler attachments, running from the back of the head toward the nasal bone. Now the antlers can be grasped and used as a lever to break the skull open lengthwise. Brain is a substance that spoils quickly, and therefore it should be fresh and processed quickly or frozen.

Since brains are not expensive, it's better to have too much on hand than too little. About 10.5 ounces of brain should be enough for a deer skin, which is more than even the smartest buck can provide. So, using an animal's brain for its own hide is very tight. It is impossible to use too much brain, but too little will result in incomplete penetration of the fibrous web with fats.

As an alternative to using brains, some tanners also use egg yolk or soap. A mixture of these two substances with the addition of a little oil has proved particularly effective. It achieves the same effect as brain, and the finished leather is indistinguishable from one tanned with brain tissue.

Tanning can also be done with other fats besides brain. Olive oil, egg yolk, and soap are good alternatives.

Preparation and heating of the fat-containing tanning solution

The fats of the egg yolk are ideal for the tanning solution.

For a fallow deer, use about twice the yolk and soap. Too much egg yolk or soap is not harmful. The oil, on the other hand, should be used sparingly, since an excess of oil will make the finished leather less airy and slightly clammy to the touch, which is due to an excessively high fat content.

Whether you use brains or the alternative mixture, the procedure that follows is the same in any case.

The substances, along with 2 cups of warm water, are placed in a sufficiently large container, such as a bucket or large bowl, and the whole is mixed with a kitchen blender until all the lumps are dissolved. The water should not be too hot if you use egg yolks, so that they are not cooked and flocculate.

Now add about a quart of hot water and mix everything again to a thin, creamy solution. Large skins need correspondingly more tanning substance and therefore more water. The temperature of the finished cocktail should be such that you can place your hands into it without scalding them. A higher temperature would also damage the skin to be tanned. The mixture can also be used cold, but in the warm state the fats are thinner and are more easily absorbed by the skin.

Before placing the hide in the tanning substance, it must first be completely wrung out.

Wringing

Wringing is an important step and is repeated several times during tanning.

If, however, the skin did not undergo the liming process and was therefore not neutralized, then it has already been sufficiently freed from wetness by the scraping process, which eliminates the need for wringing. Such a skin can be placed directly into the tanning solution.

Otherwise, the skin must first be wrung out vigorously before insertion to prepare it for absorption of the tanning solution, because a completely wet skin cannot possibly absorb more liquid.

Wringing requires a sturdy wooden pole, about the size of a broomstick, which is fixed somewhere horizontally at chest height. This can be between two trees, in a door frame, or between two pegs driven into the ground especially for this purpose. In any case, this structure should be mounted firmly enough to withstand some load. Over this crossbar, you now place the skin, from which the water has dripped off, and wrap it into a ring as shown. Another sturdy stick is used to turn the skin in one direction and wring it out vigorously. Wringing requires quite a bit of force, because the aim is to squeeze out as much liquid as possible from the fibrous structure of the hide. Even small skins prove to

A great deal of effort is required when wringing, especially with large skins.

An alternative method If you do not have a fixed crossbar for wringing

Wringing is an important work step and is shown here in its various stages.

be quite stable, and tearing of even thin skins is unlikely.

If scarcely any liquid is dripping from the skin, loosen the skin ring, move it a little in its position on the rod, insert the stick through it again, and wring again, this time preferably in the opposite direction. Proceed in this manner one or two more times until hardly any water drips from the skin. Then loosen the now badly shrunken skin ring again and stretch the skin in all directions until it has almost regained its original shape and all wrinkles have disappeared.

Now you can put it into the container with the warm tanning solution.

Application

It's not enough to just put the skin in the tanning solution and hope for a miracle. A wrung-out skin is often still wrinkled and stiff, and the edges in particular are usually crumpled and rolled up. However, in order for the skin to completely relax in the tanning solution and soak up the fats,

you have to help it along with your hands and sometimes even your feet. To do this, the skin in the container is stretched a bit, kneaded, and turned around. Large, thick skins need much more attention here than thin ones. In any case, the skin must be completely relaxed and fully soaked as before wringing. It must cling to the hands and must no longer show any hardened areas. The edges in particular require special attention. In the case of really large hides, such as those of adult red deer, it also helps to step into the container with the feet (barefoot or with rubber boots) and to work in the tanning solution by stamping and kicking. All this may take from ten minutes to half an hour. After that, take the dripping wet and limp skin out of the container and wring it out one more time. The dripping tanning solution is collected for recycling in a container placed underneath. Wringing presses the tanning substance deeper into the fibers of the skin, at the same time stretching it and also draining off excess liquid.

Should the wound skin ring ever slip apart

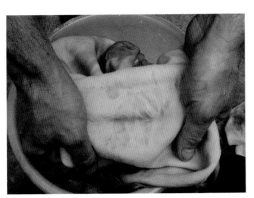

Compressed darker areas in the skin that have not absorbed tanning solution are also visually recognizable. When stretched, they disappear and also become full.

during wringing, this means that it contained too much liquid before wrapping. So you need to wring out the skin a little more by hand before you start wrapping.

Wringing is followed by stretching of the skin, after which it is again placed in the tanning solution, because soaking the skin once is rarely sufficient. If the tanning solution has cooled down in the meantime, it should be reheated beforehand.

For a fallow deer skin the process of soaking and wringing is usually repeated two or three times. Very thick and large skins require a corresponding number of repetitions.

Gradually, a change in the behavior of the skin can then be seen. It can be wrung out more completely and then also stretched more easily and farther. This is a sign that it has been completely penetrated by the fats. In addition, small bubbles or foam often form on the surface of the skin during wringing—this is a good thing, indicating that the fiber mesh is airy, open, and permeable.

For the beginner, it is recommended that the soaking and wringing be done one more time, because repeated soaking does not harm the skin. However, incomplete saturation with the fats in the tanning solution can lead to an imperfect and in places stiffened end product.

Just as you have to pay attention to certain places when scraping and also when soaking, this also applies to wringing. If, for example, wet, bluish-white areas are still noticeable on a skin that has been wrung out and stretched back to its natural size, which is often the case on thick areas, such as the end of the torso or the neck, then this is an indication of incomplete wringing of these areas. Such areas contain too much moisture to absorb further tanning substance during rewetting. Such areas should be reworked on the tanning frame with a scraper and the remaining liquid scraped out. By the way, the edges of the skin can also be smoothed out well with the scraper, should this not be sufficiently possible with bare hands.

SEWING THE HOLES

Most skins contain a few holes.

In the case of wild animals, there are usually the entry and exit holes made by the bullet. Furthermore, holes often occur during skinning of the animal and possibly also during scraping. Most of these holes can be sewn up in such a way that they are hardly noticeable in the finished leather. It is at the discretion of the tanner which holes he wants to sew up and which not. Especially the flanks and thus the thin areas of the skin often have holes. One may possibly decide to cut off the entire periphery instead of sewing them up.

In any case, sewing the holes is done after the last wringing. The skin is still moist. Before the sewing begins, ensure that the edges of the holes are clean and smooth, and trim the edges if necessary. For this purpose, you can use ordinary nail scissors.

ON A SIDE NOTE! Repair

The patching of damaged areas and the closing of holes in the leather, but especially in furs, is called "repairing" in historical jargon and was an important step in the process. In this way, with the help of many tricks of the trade, it was possible to save precious raw material.

Holes resulting from knife cuts are usually of elongated shape, in contrast to more roundish holes, such as bullet holes. All holes should be sewn along their natural course, if they have one (i.e., lengthwise). This ensures that they lie flat in the finished leather and do not cause bumps. One can make out the shape of the hole by stretching the surrounding skin in all directions. This reveals in which direction the hole lies flattest. If, on the other hand, one has holes that have arisen because a large piece of skin is missing, it is almost impossible to close them successfully

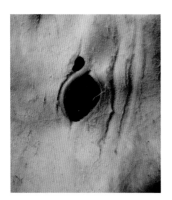  

This hole was created by a knife cut while removing the skin. The other two images show the same hole, ready for sewing and then in the finished state.

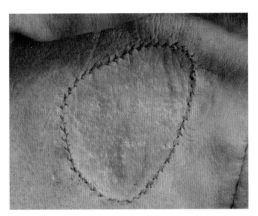

Palm-sized bullet exit holes in wild animal skins cannot be sewn up. After tanning, however, the hole can be patched, as on this shirt.

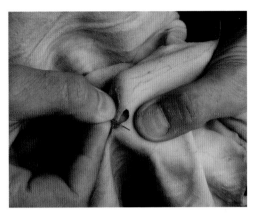

Sew holes before softening.

without the finished leather later throwing bumps. In addition, such seams can tear open again during subsequent softening. After tanning, it may be possible to place a separate piece of leather there, or you may simply have to leave the hole open.

It's necessary to use strong thread for sewing up holes, because the seams and the entire skin will be subjected to intense pulling and stretching.

Strong synthetic yarns are particularly well suited. Interestingly, dental floss, for example, is of ideal strength and thickness. For those who tan a lot and also want to sew leather, it is advisable to purchase

waxed "artificial sinew." This plastic yarn can be spliced to any fine thread yarn as desired and is very strong. Instead of a knot being tied at the end of the yarn, these synthetic yarns are joined simply by melting the ends with a lighter to form a small knot.

It's advisable to use an ordinary sewing needle and not a triangular leather needle, because the latter has a sharp point, which cuts small holes in the skin; these may later widen and appear very unsightly on the finished leather. You should do the stitching from the flesh side, since this is usually the inside of clothing and other products, making the stitching of the holes less noticeable. The finer the stitching is

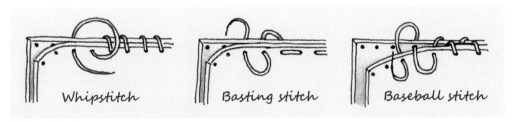

Whipstitch   Basting stitch   Baseball stitch

Various sewing stitches used in this book.

done, the less noticeable it is in the finished leather. The baseball stitch provides the strongest and neatest seam. Especially in thick places, the damp skin can be very tough and you will need a thimble or can wrap your finger with a piece of leather when sewing.

Another possibility is to guide the needle with a small pair of serrated needle-nose pliers (see "Sewing," p. 113).

All seams should be sewn very tightly to prevent loosening during softening. Generally, most seams do not lie flat immediately after sewing. However, this is of no further importance since they will stretch out in the following step of softening.

Occasionally, seams tear open during softening. If this is the case, they should be closed again immediately.

DRYING AND SOFTENING

Softening is the crucial step in the entire tanning process, creating a soft, airy leather from a wet piece of hide.

If you work outdoors, this work requires a warm, sunny day, preferably with some wind, so that the skin can dry during processing. In case of doubt, a fire can also be lit. If, on the other hand, you work indoors, you'll need an additional source of heat in the form of a stove or heater to allow the skin to dry quickly.

In this step, the skin is dried, but not by leaving it to its own devices as in the production of rawhide. Rather, it must be kept in motion during drying; otherwise, it'll become hard.

During this drying process, the skin is continuously stretched and otherwise manipulated by hand, so that so that when fin-

Softening requires heat.

ished it is beautifully supple and flexible.

This process can take an hour or more depending on the size of the skin and the prevailing temperatures.

Like scraping, softening involves some effort and physical labor, especially when working on a large or thick hide, such as that of an adult red deer. A novice may even develop blisters on his hands from the continuous forceful manipulation of large hides. Wearing gloves during this work is an option, although it significantly reduces the ability to feel the condition of the hide. Another option is to apply tape around your knuckles to protect them before starting the softening of large skins.

At the beginning of the softening process, the skin is wrung out as described above and stretched to its original size. Howev-

er, even in this state it still contains too much moisture to benefit from immediate processing. Therefore, it is first spread out in the sun to dry evenly (e.g., over a beam, a bush, or the back of a chair, or hung in front of the stove or a fire).

The fine art of softening and drying is to know how long to let the skin dry before you start working on it. If it is left too long, it will become hard and brittle in some places, and softening will no longer be possible. If, on the other hand, it is still too moist when you are working on it, you are working in vain, because the aim of softening is to prevent the fibers of the skin from sticking together and stiffening, so that they remain flexible against each other even when dry. If the skin is too wet, the fibers merely slip back and forth on top of each other, and nothing is achieved. If the skin has dried too much, the fibers are

If a few friends pitch in to help, the work is more fun and you are able to stretch the skin vigorously.

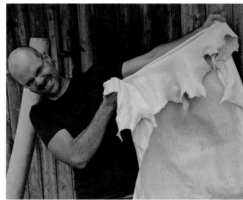

Softening can be exhausting and sometimes frustrating. The skin is stretched continuously in all directions. There is no need for a visit to the gym on such days.

already firmly glued together and remain stiff. This is aggravated by the fact that the skin is of different thickness in different places and therefore dries more quickly in some places than in others. All these factors must be taken into account when softening. For beginners, it is therefore advisable to start softening a little too soon than too late. Because once certain areas have dried hard and stiff, the only solution is to soak them again in the tanning substance. During drying, therefore, the skin should be treated with care and not exposed to excessive heat. Check its condition regularly, about every ten minutes. To do this, let it slide through your hands and feel it evenly. Are there any areas that are already beginning to harden like cardboard? As we know from the scraping process, it is also important here to direct your attention to the thinner areas on the flanks, legs, and edges. These areas dry the fastest and are therefore the first to require treatment. Thick and moist areas,

such as the torso, neck, and rump, can be disregarded for the time being.

Softening is achieved by pulling and stretching the skin by hand, for which there are different ways of working.

For example, take hold of the skin at the head end and hold it with both hands, right and left of the neck, at the edges. Now pull them apart firmly, like a chest expander in the gym. Then move your hands down a little farther and repeat the process. In this way, you stretch the entire width of the skin until the tail end is reached.

Then turn the skin 90 degrees and repeat the whole process, stretching it lengthwise in the opposite direction. This crosswise stretching is very important. In between, the skin should also be worked diagonally.

For a change, you can also stretch skins over your knees while sitting. To do this,

Stretching the skin over one knee.

A steel cable, available in hardware stores, is particularly suitable for softening skins. With a loop at each end, it's attached to a wall or door frame with sturdy hooks.

lay them spread out over your thighs, take hold of the ends on the right and left, and stretch them downward by bending forward and at the same time spreading your knees apart. If there is a clean surface, you can also stand with both feet on one end of the skin and grasp the other end with both hands to pull it upward. If, on the other hand, you have one or more or more assistants on hand, the skin can also be stretched out like a life net and pulled in opposite directions. During this stretching process, you will see that the previously roughly amber-colored skin with its relatively smooth surface stretches in many places to such an extent that the fiber mesh opens up and it changes from a beige to a white color with an airy surface, the structure of the finished leather.

There are also some tools that can be used to help make softening easier or more effi-

cient.

One of them is a strong rope, about the thickness of a pencil and about a yard long. This is attached with one end at head height and the other at waist level (i.e., vertically); for example, on a tree trunk, a beam, or a wall. The skin is placed through the resulting D-shaped loop and pulled back and forth over the rope with both hands. The skin is also worked in all directions on the rope.

This process generates additional heat, which helps with drying, and the skin is stretched more when pulled over the narrow rope than is possible by hand. In addition, the rope loosens the surface of the skin and makes it supple. As an alternative to the rope, a thin metal cable can also be used as shown.

Furthermore, for outdoor work one can use a wooden stake with embedded metal blade. The stake should be sturdy

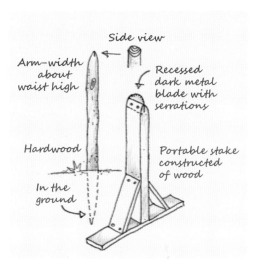

With both hands, grasp the skin and pull the 8 to 12 inches of skin between them vigorously over the cable a few times.

Stake for softening skins. On the left is a primitive variant; on the right is the mobile version.

Working with large skins may cause sore fingertips and knuckles. So it's important to vary the grip.

and therefore have a diameter of about 4 inches. It is sharpened at one end and driven vertically into the ground so that the other end is at about waist height. This is sharpened to a crescent-shaped edge. Alternatively, a thin metal blade that is also concave can be used. The whole construction can also be made of lumber with a wooden frame. The stake is thus transportable and can be used indoors. For processing, the skin is placed over the blade of the stake, grasped right and left with your hands, and pulled vigorously back and forth over the same to target the edges or particularly stubborn areas. This has approximately the same effect as the rope. Like the drawknives used for scraping, the blade need not be razor sharp, but it should have some bite.

In addition, you should get a special scraper. This is wielded with one hand and consists of a wooden handle with a recessed metal blade. This tool also requires a thin crescent-shaped blade, which can also be provided with fine serrations by filing (see photo, p. 64).

Tanners softening skins. The man in the center is using a cable, while the one on the right has a stake.

Working on a crossbeam

ON A SIDE NOTE! Alternative Tools

Various scrapers and tools for tanning can also be made without much effort from old gardening, farming, and woodworking tools; for example, from spatulas, gouges, floorboard scrapers, tree scrapers, spades, bark peelers, and the like. These are often shapely and fit well in the hand. In most cases one must rework the blade only a bit, shorten it, and give it the necessary concave shape, and the tool is ready. Treasure troves for such old tools are flea markets, junk stores, and, of course, the internet.

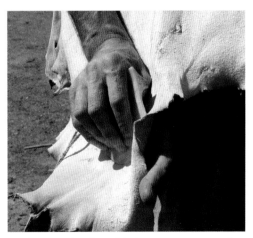

Working on the skin with the scraper to stretch and roughen it and remove crusts. This scraper is cut from the shoulder blade of a cow.

To work with this scraper, place the skin spread out over the crossbar, which was previously used for wringing, fix it there by leaning against it with the upper body and grasping and stretching the loosely hanging end with one hand, then tension, stretch, and scrape it with the scraper in the other hand with strong, even downward movements. For this purpose, the skin can also be placed over the back of a chair, for example. Then sit upside down on the chair and fix the skin with the upper part of the body, grasp the freely hanging end with one hand, stretch it out and work it vigorously with the scraper.

The scrapers are particularly suitable for removing possible crusts on the surface of the leather, which are caused by the drying process, and to give it an airy and terry cloth-like structure. When using any of these tools, feel free to "make sparks fly," which means that small fuzzy pieces of skin are removed.

This is quite desirable, since it opens up the surface of the skin and makes it soft and supple and, at the same time, promotes drying. If you have now worked the skin continuously for some time, you can leave it in the sun or in the oven for a while and let it dry further. This will give you a few minutes to catch your breath. If, on the other hand, you need a longer break, place the skin in a plastic bag and put it in a cool place. This protects it from drying out further. As already mentioned, attention is first directed to the thin areas of the skin, to work on them through targeted stretching until they are dry and soft. The outermost few millimeters of the edge can often never be completely softened and are simply cut off after smoking.

While you are working on the edges and the thin flanks, you must not ignore the rest of the skin. Places that already feel a little unyielding and stiffened like cardboard need special attention. Stubborn, unyielding areas can best be softened by vigorous working them with the stake or rope. Softening is a process that literally requires dexterity, since the hands are used to continuously scan the skin, feeling and searching for the next areas that will require work.

The nape of the neck, places along the backbone, and the area above the tail (the buttocks of the animal) are the thickest areas of any skin. They require the most work at the end of the process, while the flanks are already dried and soft, and are usually the ones that are the most difficult to

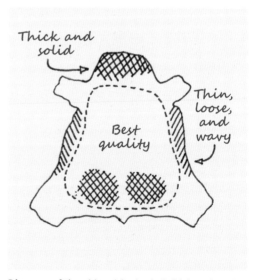

Diagram of the skin with shaded thick and stubborn areas as well as thin and flexible areas. These differences are noticeable during scraping, softening and processing of the finished leather.

soften and occasionally even remain stiff. If hard spots remain in an otherwise soft hide, which cannot be removed despite aggressive processing, then there is no alternative, and the hide must be placed in the tanning substance again and the softening process repeated. Here, too, it is experience that teaches you to recognize at an early stage whether a hide requires further treatment with the tanning substance or not.

Work on the skin should not be completely stopped until it is completely dry and one hopes soft, white, and supple.

SMOKING

This last step of the tanning process described here is smoking; however, it is not absolutely necessary. Many Native American tribes, for example, are known to use white unsmoked leather for ceremonial clothing, in part because it provides a better contrast as a background for paintings and decorations. However, when this leather gets wet, it loses its suppleness after drying and becomes stiff and rough, so the process of softening has to be repeated (although with much less effort).

However, in order to obtain a serviceable leather that may be dampened or even washed and be as supple afterward as before, it is necessary to smoke the white hide after softening.

This process gives the leather a golden yellow to brown color, and it retains its suppleness even after repeated wetting. In addition, the smoke odor has a beneficial effect against insects (see p. 84), which occasionally attack raw hides, white leather, and furs if they are stored for too long in

Schematic of a smoking device for two equal-size leathers

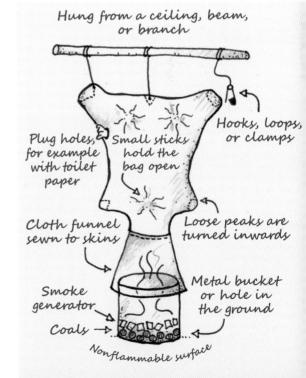

Hung from a ceiling, beam, or branch

Plug holes, for example with toilet paper

Small sticks hold the bag open

Hooks, loops, or clamps

Cloth funnel sewn to skins

Loose peaks are turned inwards

Smoke generator

Metal bucket or hole in the ground

Coals →

Nonflammable surface

dark, poorly ventilated places.

For smoking, a kind of bag is formed from the leather, into which the smoke is directed.

The Smoking Bag

If you have only one skin to smoke, fold it lengthwise, along the backbone. If you want to smoke two hides, which is more economical because of the amount of work involved, choose two hides of the same size and approximately the same thickness and place them congruently on top of each other. To form the skins into a tightly sealed bag, from which as little smoke as possible should escape, the skins are sewn together along the outer edge. Only the neck is not sewn closed, because smoke will be introduced through this opening.

The sewing can be done by hand with an ordinary stitch, or the seam can be sewn with a sewing machine. Sewing by hand is more time consuming, and if you have an ordinary household sewing machine, you should use it. There is no need for a spe-cial leather needle for this work. A wide, loose stitch width and the use of a thread with low tensile strength are recommend-ed, since the sewn bag will be torn open again along the seam at the end of the smoking process. If, on the other hand, the stitch width is too narrow and the thread too tight, it can happen with thin skins that the skin tears along the seam when the bag is torn open.

The edges of the leather should match each other as closely as possible, but small points and protrusions are no prob-lem. They can be sewn in or cut off. Holes in the leather that were not sewn up be-fore softening also represent no problem. However, they should be plugged during smoking to prevent excessive smoke from escaping. The less smoke that escapes from the leather bag, the faster the pro-cess is completed.

The Fabric Funnel

A tubular funnel made of fabric is used to create a space between the smoke source and the leather and guide the smoke into the leather bag. For this purpose, one makes a funnel approximately 20 inches in length from a solid piece of cloth, such as denim or canvas. It is advisable not to use synthetic fibers, since this increases the risk of fire. This funnel is attached to the leather bag, with its smaller opening

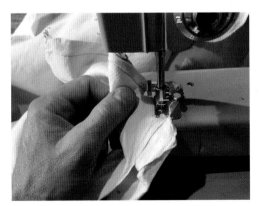

Brain-tanned leather can be sewn wonderfully with an ordinary sewing machine. The smoking bag can also be made in this way.

Smoking material and smoking bucket made from a large tin can. In the foreground is willow bark, while behind it is brown rotten wood.

placed over the opening in the neck of the bag, and sewn there. The wider end should be large enough to fit loosely over the container in which the smoke is generated.

The Smoking Bucket

Smoke is generated in a vessel and then fed into the leather bag. For this purpose, one uses a metal bucket of about 12 to 20 inches in diameter or a similar fireproof vessel. In the smoking bucket a fire is lit or charcoal is ignited. Once this has created a properly glowing bed of coals that covers the entire bottom of the bucket, the smoking material is added to create dense, acrid smoke. Instead of a bucket, one can, for example, use a wood-burning stove, feeding the smoke through the stovepipe into the leather bag. Only smoke should be produced in the smoking bucket, with no open flames.

The Smoking Material

In principle, any naturally combustible material that produces smoke can be used as a smoking material; for example, leaves, hay or straw, coarse sawdust, wood chips,

Smoker setup for two deerskins. The bag is hanging in a structure made of four spruce poles. The outside is already golden brown. There is no smoke to be seen. This is how it should be, since it means that the bag is tight.

even cow or sheep dung. In any case, the material should be well dried, and it's important to bear in mind that leaves and hay turn to ash more quickly than bark, for example, and therefore must be available in larger quantities. The preferred smoking material, however, is rotten wood; namely, that of dead trees, the interior of which has been attacked by so-called brown rot. This damage, which is caused by fungal infestation, leads to a reddish-brown discoloration of the wood, which disintegrates into angular pieces—so-called brown cubical rot. This rotting wood is collected and the pieces are reduced to about the size of ordinary grilling charcoal, after which they are air-dried in prior to use.

Rotten wood from conifers should not contain resin crumbs, since they produce soot and can stick to the surface of the leather. The wood should also not be so moldy that it completely crumbles and breaks into fine fibers when touched. Different smoking materials produce different colors of leather.

This smoking device is located in a shed. The skins are hanging from the ceiling. Under the smoking bucket is a fireproof plate. Here you are protected from the wind and rain.

Taking apart the smoking bag. If you use thin, weak yarn, the bag is easy to tear open. The leather is ready!

The Process

Smoking can be done in the open air, but you should make sure that there is no danger of rain and that it is relatively windless. Working under a roof or even in a shed or shelter, on the other hand, is safer, because there you are independent of wind and weather. The leather bag is hung so that the fabric funnel can fall over the smoking bucket to direct the resulting smoke into the bag. The smoking bag with the attached funnel can be hung from a branch, canopy, or any other stable structure. The key is to keep the smoking bag open by inserting two to four thin sticks or wood chips to allow the smoke to circulate freely inside. These sticks should then be repositioned two to three times to ensure even smoking. In addition, you can help from the outside by inserting small hooks

(e.g., bent pins) through the leather and fastening them somewhere with string to keep the bag somewhat stretched and open, because if the insides of the bag touch, no smoke can reach them there, and these spots will remain white.

Holes in the skins can be plugged with dry grass, toilet paper, or rags to prevent excessive smoke from escaping.

Now sprinkle a few handfuls of smoking material on the bed of coals, and in no time a dense acrid smoke develops. This is exactly what is needed. No flames, just a lot of smoke!

One should be present during the entire smoking process and regularly check the contents of the bucket. There should be

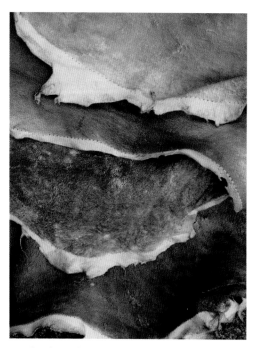

Two leathers that were smoked for different lengths of time with resulting color differences. The duration of smoking and the type of smoking material are responsible for the color.

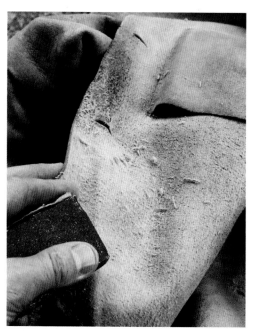

Instead of constantly washing your finished leather products, it is better to remove superficial dirt with coarse sandpaper, as in the case of this old and well-worn leather jacket.

no flames flaring up, which could scorch the fabric funnel or even the leather. To do this, occasionally lift the hopper at one point, peek into the bucket, and feel for hot spots with a hand inserted into the bucket. If flames develop, you can spray them with some water, which you should always have on hand, or you can add a little more moist smoking material. If the smoke development subsides, you must add a little more smoking material.

Duration of Smoking

Usually, you start by smoking the hair side of the skins. If, after some time, a brownish discoloration appears on the flanks or oth-

er thin areas on the outside of the leather (i.e., the flesh side), this means that the smoke has already completely penetrated the skin there, and it can be assumed that the hair side has been sufficiently smoked. Alternatively, check the progress of the smoking process or the discoloration of the skin by pulling the fabric funnel from the bucket, turning it up to the neck, and thus looking at the leather bag from the inside. If there are larger holes in the leather, the plugs can be removed, and through these openings you can check the discoloration process inside the bag. The duration of the smoking process depends on the size of the skins and therefore the volume of the bag and the intensity of the smoke development, and for a bag made of two fallow deer skins it can be between fifteen minutes and one hour.

Once one side is smoked, turn the leather bag with the funnel inside out and smoke the other side for the same amount of time. Then remove the funnel and tear the smoking bag along the seam. Done!

Smoking devices other than those described here, such as those used for meat or fish, in which the hung product is smoked in the open, have proved to be unsuitable, since while several skins can be smoked at once, the duration of the smoking process is much longer because the smoke merely brushes over the free-hanging hides and does not penetrate them so easily. But of course, one can experiment with such methods.

The color of freshly smoked leather depends on the length of the smoking process and the choice of smoking material. A longer smoke always results in a darker shade. However, this coloration is not lightfast, because when the leather is exposed to sunlight it fades continually over the months.

Washing and Cleaning

At first, smoked skins smell strongly of smoke, which after washing and longer airing can be reduced to a pleasant level. It is therefore recommended that you wash the leather after smoking. This not only reduces the smell of smoke but also removes any residue from smoking that occasionally gives the surface a slightly sticky feel. In addition, washing gives the skin the opportunity to rest in its natural form after the structurally punishing softening process.

Smoked leather or clothing made from it can be washed by hand using cold or lukewarm water and a little mild soap.

Afterward, the leather should be carefully wrung out and laid flat to dry. Hanging on a clothesline is not suitable for heavy and thicker skins until the leather has already dried; otherwise the leather or garment will lose its shape.

Once the garment or leather is almost completely dry, it should be shaken out gently and stretched a bit to allow the leather to regain its natural shape. Subsequent roughening of the surface with pumice or coarse sandpaper can finish the process, to give the surface its maximum velvetiness. Constant and repeated washing should be avoided, however, since the suppleness of the skins may suffer in the long run. Instead, as with wool garments, extensive airing and occasional "sunbathing" are preferable. Crusty, greasy, and other types of soiling should therefore be removed by brushing or sanding. Coarse sandpaper for woodworking or coarse wire brushes used for removing rust and the like are also suitable for this purpose. The surfaces of leather objects can be cleaned and renewed with even circular and criss-cross movements.

TANNING PELTS

The following chapter describes the tanning of pelts; that is, skins with the hair coat intact. The skins of the various ungulates such as roe deer, chamois, goat, and sheep, but also from large animals such as elk, cattle, and bison, can be processed in this way. However, very large hides in particular require a correspondingly greater amount of work and are therefore not recommended as beginner's projects. As already mentioned at the start, the method discussed here is not particularly suitable for wild boar hides.

But before tackling a pelt from a full-grown red deer, you should already have some experience with the production of leather and have tanned some smaller hides, since it is a very labor-intensive process, which without the necessary practice can be very frustrating. All data in this section refer to an average-sized fallow deer skin. To anyone particularly interested in tanning very large hides such as beef, elk, or bison, I recommend the author's book *Native American Buffalo Robes* (see "Further Reading," p. 134).

Many of the skills that are necessary for processing a pelt have already been taught in the chapter "The Basics of Tanning Leather" (see p. 40) and will not be repeated here. Therefore, it is advisable to first read this chapter thoroughly and internalize it.

Of course, there are also many differences compared to leather production, and these are described in detail below.

One of the main features of the tanning of pelts, as opposed to leather, is to prevent the hair from falling out during the process. Wherever persistent moisture and heat come together, there lurks the danger of bacterial development and thus hair loss. What is desirable for the production of leather must be avoided here. This means that the aforementioned liming step is omitted during the processing of pelts.

In addition to the criteria mentioned in the chapter The Practice under "The Selection, Procurement, and Quality of Raw Materials," p. 27, it is important to note that, especially with salted hides, there is always a risk that bacterial development has set in and that, as a result, the hairs will come out in one place or another, despite all precautions. The same danger also exists with dried skins, especially thick ones, because these must first be soaked for a considerable time to make them flexible. Basically, fresh or freshly frozen skins are best suited.

ON A SIDE NOTE! Insect Infestation

Watch out for insect infestation! Since the method described here is an ecological process that does not require aggressive chemicals, pelts and furs, as well as clothing made of wool, remain an interesting food for insects such as moths and fur beetles. However, this is a problem only if the skins or items made from them lie around unused for a long time in dark and poorly ventilated places, such as chests, drawers, or cupboards. Insect pests love such places, and their larvae mainly gnaw the epidermis, causing hair loss. They do not pose a threat to leather. So, if skins are to be stored for a longer period of time, it is recommended that you pack them in tightly sealable containers or thick plastic bags. Even better are tightly sealed cloth bags, which still allow the skins to "breathe." The addition of rags soaked in essential oils or whole plant parts is also helpful. Historically, in this country, camphor, clove root, tansy, and iris were mainly used for this purpose, but also lavender and cedar. Furthermore, in the past sulfur and borax were used to control insects but are now excluded because of the health hazard. Fumigation also has a deterrent effect on insects.

Occasional airing in the sun and a process called "knocking" using specially prepared hazelnut rods, which are beaten on the skins in a certain rhythm, was once the predominant method used by furriers to remove insect larvae and dirt from valuable furs.

WASHING

All skins should be thoroughly washed before processing. The hair side in particular requires some attention to rinse out dirt, blood, or other impurities. Warm water mixed with soap or detergent is best used for this purpose. Washing is especially important when using salted hides.

Such skins must be thoroughly rinsed and soaked until all salt has been washed out. Depending on the degree of contamination, the water will need to be changed several times until the wash water ideally remains clear.

THE RACK AND RACKING

The second major difference from leather tanning is that the pelts are placed in a rack for processing. Racking a pelt directly on the ground, with the help of pegs, as known from ethnology, is unsuitable for the modern tanner in most cases.

Square timbers from the hardware store are particularly suitable for the construction of a mobile rack. For a deer skin, the timbers should have an edge dimension of about 1.6 x 2.4 inches or a comparable thickness. It is always advisable to build a rack that is too sturdy rather than one that is too weak, because it will be subjected to stresses during stretching, drying, and processing of the pelt, and these stresses will be greater the larger and thicker the hide. For the construction of the rack, the ends of the squared lumber can be provided with notches that fit into one another, resulting in a sturdier structure.

Then join the beams together by using sturdy nails or screws. The use of wing screws is recommended if you want to disassemble the rack after use; for example, to save storage space. Of course, rustic rack variants can also be made; for example, from unprocessed spruce logs or the like. Cross braces across the corners of the rack are also recommended for reinforce-

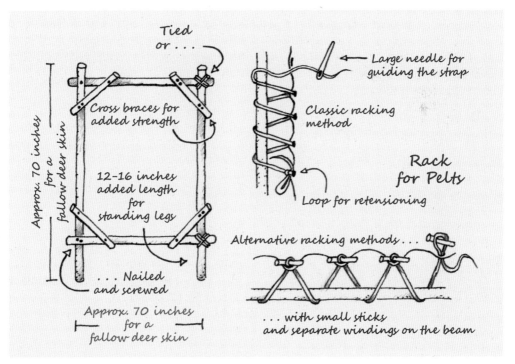

Rack design and racking methods for tanning pelts

Constructing a rack from dry spruce

A homemade needle, like this one made of bone, can be used to thread the cord through the holes in the skin before stretching it in the rack.

ment. It is also worth constructing a rack with support legs (i.e., leaving the vertical timbers in the lower section longer than necessary) to provide a more comfortable working position for later processing of the skin.

The rack must be quite a bit larger than the fresh skin. This is necessary because the skin expands in all directions during binding as well as processing.

For a fallow deer skin, the distance between the edge of the skin and the beam should therefore be about 8 inches on all sides. This results in a rack about 48 inches wide and 60 inches long. However, because of the support legs, the vertical beams should be about an additional 12 to

16 inches longer.

Once the rack is finished, the pelt is placed in the center, and holes are made around the edge for securing it to the frame.

For hides the size of a fallow deer, the distance between the individual holes should be about 2.5 to 3 inches. For larger skins they can be farther apart, and for smaller skins the distance is reduced accordingly. This is necessary to better distribute the stresses on the individual holes during stretching and processing. Very thin pelts, such as winter blankets made from deerskin, nevertheless have a tendency to occasionally tear out at the holes during processing. If this happens, all you have to do is cut a new hole next to the affected area

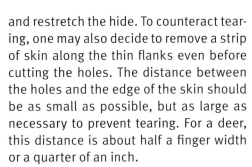

The winter coat of a fallow deer, racked and fully stretched

Sturdy racks and correspondingly strong cords or cables are necessary for very large skins, such as this one from a bison.

and restretch the hide. To counteract tearing, one may also decide to remove a strip of skin along the thin flanks even before cutting the holes. The distance between the holes and the edge of the skin should be as small as possible, but as large as necessary to prevent tearing. For a deer, this distance is about half a finger width or a quarter of an inch.

The easiest way to cut the holes is to lay the skin on the ground with the flesh side up. Now push a board under the edge of the skin and then pierce through the skin with a knife from above, against the resistance of the board. In some places along the edge, you may have to remove with a knife any meat or fat residue before doing this. In the case of particularly thick skins, such as beef, bison, or elk, the skin should be split horizontally with the knife in particularly thick places, such as the neck, before the holes are made and thus thinned out. Once all the holes have been cut in the skin, the hide is tied tightly into the center of the rack with sturdy cord or rope.

Thick cord distributes the forces acting on the clamping holes better than thin cord and thus also helps prevent the holes from being torn out. The cord should have a diameter of at least 0.10 inches. For large and thick skins, correspondingly stronger cords or ropes are necessary. Racking requires more cord than one might expect at first glance. So, for a deer skin, you should have at least 5 feet of cord ready. This can also be cut into two or more pieces to make racking easier, since this prevents the risk of tangling while working. To begin with, the skin is first tied loosely into the rack evenly and centrally, according to its natural shape. Only then is it tightened all around until the skin is tight and no longer has any creases.

If you use relatively thin cords, it can be helpful to use a large needle to guide the cord through the cut holes. Such a needle can also be made from wood, bone, or metal. The cord should always be fed through the holes from the flesh side. This prevents hair from being carried along when the string is pulled through, which can clog the hole and make it difficult to pull through.

FLESHING AND DRYING

After clamping, the rack is lifted from the ground and leaned vertically against a wall so that the following processing can be done standing up. Now it is first necessary to remove all large fat and meat residues from the skin. This is easily done with bare hands or with the aid of a sharp knife.

Smaller remnants and thinnest tissue layers can remain on the skin for the time being, since they do not hinder the subsequent drying process. Depending on the condition and size of the hide, this work can be completed in just a few minutes. On the other hand, removing the flesh from a large bison hide can take several hours.

When fleshing a skin that has been racked, large contiguous layers can be removed with bare hands to ensure rapid drying of the underlying skin.

During the fleshing process, the skin usually gives a little and may sag. Therefore, it must be retightened before the following drying. Drying can then be done outdoors, weather permitting. This may require several days before a large deer hide is completely dry. However, direct and extreme sunlight should be avoided. It is safest to place the frame under a roof in a shelter, garage, or barn. Adequate ventilation should be provided in enclosed spaces and for large skins. It may also be necessary to have an additional heat source on hand, such as a wood stove or gas heater, to ensure rapid drying. If moisture persists for a long time, there is a risk of rotting, resulting in the loss of hair, or the skin even begins to mold.

In winter, hides can also be freeze-dried outdoors if sub-zero temperatures are reliably sustained.

Once the hide is stiffly dried and thus tight as a drum, it's safe from bacterial attack and decay, and the following scraping can now be done at will.

REMOVAL OF THE SUBCUTIS AND THINNING

In this step the subcutis and remaining tissue and fat are removed, thus preparing the hide for the subsequent tanning process. Various types of tools are suitable for this work. What they all have in common, however, is a convexly curved narrow working edge, similar to that used for softening leather, and a handle that fits well in the hand. Razor-sharp blades made of high-quality tool steel are ideal, but reworked spatulas or even tools made of bone and flint, as known from archeology, also prove to be amazingly effective if one is familiar with their use. The scraper is held with one hand and applied to the skin at an angle of 45°. With pressure, the tool is pulled evenly over the skin from top to bottom to remove the dry tissue from the flesh side.

Tools for removing subcutaneous tissue from dried skins. *From left*: scraper made from the metatarsal (lower leg bone) of a red deer, flat chisel, iron blade in wooden handle with fine serrations, flint scraper (Latin *silex*) in a wooden handle. All of these tools have a narrow concave working edge.

Mode of operation when removing the subcutis. The blade is placed at a right angle to the skin and pulled downward, creating the typical scrapings.

In some places, the dried subcutis can also be peeled off by hand. But be careful in thin areas, since the whole skin can tear with it.

Working position when removing the subcutis. The scraping of this skin is virtually complete.

It is not easy for the novice to see how much material has to be removed or how deep he must scrape, since compared to the wet-scraping method for leather described above, it is preferable to work with very sharp tools, which can also remove too much material.

However, the tissue to be removed has a coarser, more fibrous, and looser structure than the underlying dermis. Experience and close observation teach when sufficient material has been removed. Occasionally, the subcutaneous tissue can also be removed in some places in coherent, parchment-like pieces, like a Band-Aid. This makes it possible to perceive the natural dividing line between the layers and to proceed accordingly. Here, too, a systematic approach should be taken to remove the entire subcutis. However, if small remnants remain in places or if the surface appears irregular and fibrous, this is not a big problem, since such areas can still be removed with an emery block or scraper during the following work steps. For maximum efficiency the blade will have to be resharpened occasionally.

Course participants using fling tools to scrape a chamois hide.

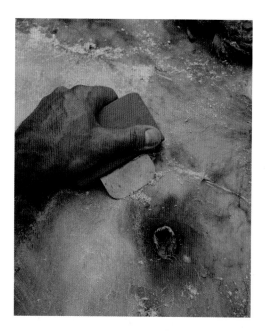

Thinning thick places produces handfuls of skin scrapings. The Indians saved these scrapings to make soup from them in hard times.

Left: With small and thin skins there is often not much tissue to remove, making it possible to use a wider scraper. The bullet entry hole is visible in this deerskin.

Particularly on the flanks, which can be as thin as paper when dry, there is a danger of damaging the skin as a result of the blade slipping sideways or by applying too much pressure.

Care should also be taken when working on the edges and the stretching holes, since one cut can be enough to sever the cords that hold the skin in the rack. If there are other holes in the skin, special care must be taken when scraping around them, so as not to enlarge them unintentionally.

On the other hand, however, in certain areas of large skins it may be necessary not only to scrape off the subcutis, but also to remove some of the underlying dermis. After all, the tanning substance is applied only from the flesh side, and there is also no skin breakdown, as in the case of leather production, to facilitate penetration of the fats, so it is advisable that particularly thick areas be scraped a little thinner before tanning, to facilitate the subsequent softening or even make it possible in the first place. In the case of fallow deer, this would basically be the areas around the rump. With full-grown red deer this also includes the neck area. With correspondingly large skins, these thick areas can be quite extensive and even cover the entire skin surface, as for example, with bison. When thin-scraping, it is especially important to have a razor-sharp blade, because now the material is really being planed off. The chips produced in the process are quite reminiscent of the wood shavings created during woodworking. As a general rule, the thinner the skin is scraped, the easier and faster the tanning and softening process. However, it is important to ensure to scrape the skin as evenly as possible, so as not to create overly thin areas, since

Thinning very large skins is correspondingly time-consuming and calls for the use of larger, two-hand scrapers.

the stresses caused by the softening process can result in holes. The naturally thin material on the flanks can be used as a reference. Since it is not possible to make objective thickness measurements of a skin, it is advisable that you estimate the thickness of the skin in different places by feeling the surface of the skin as well as lightly tapping and palpating it, including from the skin side. Here too, with experience one gains confidence in deciding how thin an entire skin or certain areas must be scraped to ensure optimum softness and, at the same time, the integrity of the skin.

DRESSING

The complete removal of the subcutis and any necessary thin-scraping of the skin is followed by the application of the tanning substance. The application of the tanning substance is carried out as described above for leather processing. For the following work steps, the hide remains in the rack. It is now placed on the floor with the flesh side up for application of the tanning solution. The surface on which the rack is placed should be level and free of bumps, since otherwise the applied solution will run off or not reach certain areas.

If you do not want the surface under the rack to be contaminated by overflowing liquid, you should place a tarpaulin or something similar under the rack. Now begin applying the warm tanning substance by hand on the flesh side and, using circular motions, distribute and rub it in evenly. Work over the entire surface in this way until all areas are evenly moistened with the liquid.

After about half an hour, the entire flesh side is then additionally treated with cloth sheets or several towels, which have been soaked in water. This prevents the skin from drying out prematurely and ensures

The tanning substance is applied to the scraped flesh side by hand.

Right: Scrapers for processing fur. At this stage, mainly scrapers with wider curved blades are used to remove excess liquid and to stretch the pelt. A seashell, a shoulder blade from a deer, or an ordinary ladle can also be used.

a reservoir of moisture. The sheets are soaked in warm water and should be applied dripping wet and wrinkle-free on the flesh side. In this state, the pelt is left to rest for several hours or overnight. After that, the sheets or towels are removed, and the rack is placed upright again. The skin should now have taken on a bluish-white color and should be hanging in the rack, completely soaked, heavy and floppy. Some hard areas not completely softened are often still present, but these do not pose a problem for the time being, since the soaking is repeated. Now the pelt is worked vigorously with the scraper from the flesh side. This serves to scrape excess liquid from the skin and drain it off. It is also stretched. Now you will also recognize which areas have absorbed less fluid. These are pulled and stretched by intensive scraping and prepared for a repeated application of the tanning substance. The edges also require special attention, since they generally do not soften as easily as the rest of the skin.

The pelt will now sag a little and can be tightened all around.

The goal is to scrape the skin until no more liquid escapes and the surface can be roughened somewhat with the scraper, which is a sign that the surface is beginning to dry. As with the wringing process in the production of leather, further application of the tanning liquid only makes sense when the skin is no longer dripping wet. Reheat the remaining tanning substance and apply it a second time, noting that quite a bit more liquid is absorbed by the roughened surface. Again, cover the skin with wet cloths and leave it for a few hours in the horizontal position. In this

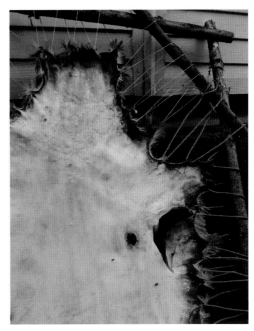

This fur has torn due to vigorous use of the scraper. Working vigorously is necessary when softening, but be careful on the thin flanks.

condition, you can also work it with your feet and walk around on the entire surface, which helps to further incorporate the liquid into the structure.

Then repeat the process of scraping described above, working the skin until it is almost dry. A sunny to semi-shaded place with good air circulation or, if necessary, an additional heat source is suitable for this. Again and again, stretch and expand the pelt vigorously with the tool, back and forth in all directions, and in between repeatedly roughen the surface to ensure faster drying. The edges in particular must be worked, since crusts tend to form here. As with the softening process in leather tanning, you do not need to work nonstop but can also let the hide dry in between and then work it vigorously again for ten to fifteen minutes. The hide will now also expand again and can be slightly retightened, but not tight like a drum, because for the following softening it should always give a little.

Be careful when stretching and expanding in thin areas, near knife cuts, or where the skin still feels slightly stiff—since the skin can tear here. To avoid tearing, instead of applying the tool by pulling vertically, you can also guide it at an acute angle and then pushing to cause stretching. When the skin is almost dry but still feels cool due to the remaining moisture, the rest of the tanning substance is applied and the process repeated once more. Soak, let rest, scrape out excess liquid, let dry, scrape, let dry, scrape, etc. In total, soaking three times should be sufficient for skins up to deer size.

SOFTENING AND SEWING HOLES

After the final soaking and before the final softening, it is necessary to sew up any holes that may be present. The skin remains in the rack for this purpose. Larger holes that cannot be closed during sewing must remain open and can be patched later, when the pelt is finished. The procedure for sewing is basically the same as described in the leather production process.

The pelt also remains in the rack for softening after the final soak. Softening is carried out, as described in the previous paragraph, by forcefully stretching and expanding the pelt over its entire area with the aid of the scraper. As an alternative to the one-handed scraper, a second scraper can also be constructed that has a sufficiently long handle to be wielded with both hands and thus more powerfully.

When softening, a sharp edge is no longer necessary, and occasionally it's even dangerous. Therefore, you either blunt the blade of your scraper or build another one, which is used only for softening skins. Especially toward the end of the softening process, when the skin has already dried to a large extent, there is a danger of it tearing due to too much pressure; on the other hand, some force is necessary to stretch it sufficiently. This balancing act can be a challenge, especially with thinner skins.

Moreover, a pelt will never become quite as supple as a leather, since the epidermis remains intact in the case of the pelt, and this prevents it from achieving comparable elasticity. However, the structure of the epidermis is broken up somewhat, which can become noticeable acoustically as a kind of crunch or crackle at the very end of the softening process during the powerful strokes with the scraper. This is a sound that the tanner is waiting for. It is an indication that the hide is now dry and well worked through. In fact, if the ominous crackling sound can be heard over the entire surface while scraping, the job is done. If the hide is dry but not supple enough at the end of the soaking process, the soaking and softening process can be repeated a second time until the desired effect is achieved.

At the very end, the flesh side can be evenly finished with coarse sandpaper to remove any remaining tissue residue and unevenness. The hair side can be combed or brushed. Finally, remove the pelt from the rack. To do this, either cut it out of the rack along the edge, leaving the slightly stiffer tension holes in the rack, or loosen the cords and leave the entire edge intact.

Stretching the pelt during softening

A two-handed scraper can also be used for softening. A spade with a rounded blade is an ideal tool. The T-shaped handle can be placed on the shoulder, which allows you to apply more pressure and relieves strain on the arms.

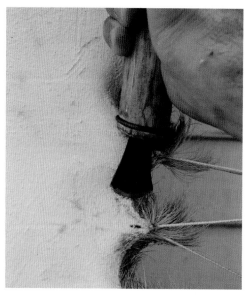

As with leather, here too the edges demand special attention since crusts tend to form there, making stretching difficult. Be careful with sharp scrapers so you don't cut the cords used to stretch the hide.

SMOKING PELTS

The smoking of pelts follows the same principles as smoking leather. Sewing them together is a little more complicated because the presence of the hairs can make the process slightly more difficult. The only difference compared to leather is that, of course, only the flesh side is smoked. The smoke therefore does not penetrate as far into the skin structure, so subsequent washing is not recommended. Basically, pelts that are used inside the house or where there is no danger of the flesh side getting wet do not need to be smoked at all. On the other hand, smoking has a deterrent effect on insect infestation by moths and fur beetles but does not permanently deter them if the skins are stored suboptimally.

Occasionally, at the end of the process a large fur can also be taken out of the rack and pulled over the rope or cable.

TANNING FURS

With regard to the tanning of furs, the chapters "The Basics of Tanning Leather" (p. 40) and "Tanning Pelts" (p. 83) should first be read and internalized, since many work steps necessary for tanning furs are described there in detail.

This section therefore deals only with processes that additionally apply to the processing of furs.

Fur-bearing animals in this country include mainly predatory game, such as fox, raccoon, marten, badger, and skunk, but also rodents, such as hares, beaver, muskrat, and nutria. Beaver and badger have very thick skins in relation to their body size. Beaver pelts must therefore often first be scraped thin in the dried state before tanning, as described in the chapter "Tanning Pelts" (p. 89). Unfortunately, this is not possible in the case of the badger, since its hide structure is similar to that of the pig and is therefore also referred to as rind. In badgers, the hair roots are very deep in the skin, and thinning the flesh side would cut through these and lead to hair loss.

Thinning the head area of a large dried beaver pelt

Tanning badger rinds by using the method described here is therefore very laborious and never results in a truly soft and supple product.

ON A SIDE NOTE! Making "Smoked Goods"

Fine, unprocessed furs and pelts are also called *Rauchware* (smoked goods) in the furrier's jargon, which finds its origin in the German words for "rough" or "raw" and has nothing to do with the fact that furs were smoked. Furthermore, when preparing furs and sometimes also pelts, one speaks of "dressing" instead of tanning.

WASHING

Washing fresh furs is not absolutely necessary but is recommended if they are badly soiled. In addition, some animal species, such as martens, skunks, and badgers, as well as male foxes during the mating season, have a rather strong body odor. This does not disappear even after tanning and would adhere to the fur permanently. The addition of essential oils to the tanning solution and a final smoking can help to some extent, but in such cases proper washing before tanning is advisable.

To do this, use lukewarm water with the addition of fat-dissolving agents, such as dishwashing or laundry detergent. The odor is largely located in the body fat of the animal, so this must be thoroughly washed out of the fur and skin.

This requires rinsing several times, each time with fresh, warm water. Washing is done in an appropriately sized bucket in which the fur is soaked, panned, kneaded, and stretched. Washing can be done before the flesh is removed, but better still after.

FLESHING

Removing the flesh from furs follows the principles described for the production of leather. The same tool, the paring knife, may even be used. The furs of larger animals, such as fox, badger, or raccoon, are scraped on the tanning beam. If the pelt was removed using the open method, a towel can be placed between the tanning beam and the pelt to protect the hair coat. Removing the flesh from the legs and the head, in particular, is very time consuming. Around the ears, eyes, and lips you will occasionally have to use a knife to remove tissue remnants. Removal of the flesh must be done very conscientiously, since, after all, the quality of the finished product is highly dependent on it. Also, great care must be taken with particularly thin furs, which can easily be damaged by the scraper. The belly area of foxes in particular is very delicate. Beaver and badger, on the other hand, have a consistently robust and dense skin structure.

If you plan to tan furs occasionally, it is worth building a separate, smaller tanning beam for this purpose. This has basically the same shape and characteristics as the large tanning beam, but because of its smaller size it is mounted on a frame where you work sitting down. Its upper end is rounded, so the pelt can be fixed by means of a ring of twisted rope or wicker.

Smaller animals, such as marten or skunk, can also be scraped on the floor, using either a board or even an inverted wooden bowl or similar article as a base. During scraping, the small furs are held in position by a nail through the nose or by just the tanner's foot. Often, an appropriately sized knife is also sufficient for scraping. Some animals have a skin that contains a great deal of fat, especially in winter. While removing the flesh, it is also important to scrape out as much of this fat as possible.

Fleshing a fox pelt with a drawknife on a small fleshing beam

The small fleshing beam. The work surface is slightly rounded. The structure must be of sturdy construction and not wobble during use.

A ring like this one is used to secure the pelt to the beam for scraping. This one is woven from willow bark.

SEWING UP THE HOLES

If there are holes in the furs, they are sewn shut after removing the flesh. Even large holes are then no longer visible from the hair side. Smaller holes, on the other hand, do not necessarily need to be sewn, since they are not noticeable anyway due to the dense coat.

DRESSING

As with pelts, the tanning substance is applied and incorporated only from the flesh side.

If you work with brains, it is recommended that you use about 7 ounces of brains for the furs of fox, badger, or raccoon, and correspondingly less for smaller animals. Otherwise, mix six egg yolks with 1 to 2 tablespoons of oil and 2 tablespoons of grated soap for the large furs and correspondingly less for the small ones.

If you are tanning a fox skin, for example, dissolve all the ingredients in about a third of a quart of warm water. If you are working with very greasy hides, you should reduce the additional use of oil to a minimum or do without it altogether.

The mixture is then massaged into the flesh side by hand, in the case of previously dried furs until the skin is flexible again. After that, place a damp, warm cloth over it and roll up the fur. Now leave the solution to act for several hours or overnight. For this purpose, the fur can be stored in a tub or a plastic bag. After that, remove the excess liquid, for example with a cloth, and begin to stretch the fur by hand. Again, warm, sunny weather or a heat source is required. Then, when the fur begins to dry a bit, apply the tanning mixture a second time and proceed as before, reducing the exposure time to about 20 to 30 minutes. For fox or rabbit pelts, three such passes are usually sufficient. Animals with thicker skin, such as badgers, raccoons, and martens, require four to five passes.

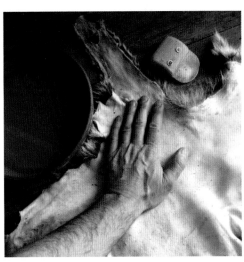

The tanning substance is spread by hand over the entire flesh side and rubbed in.

SOFTENING

After the final soaking with the tanning solution, the skin is worked continuously until completely dry. Here, the rope and the stake are used again, as already described in "The Basics of Tanning Leather". Caution is required with thin furs, such as fox. This is because the very sensitive skin on the belly in particular can tear very easily if treated too aggressively. It is possible that hairs may be pulled out through the flesh side of raccoon and badger pelts while working on the pole and rope. This is not a big deal, since dozens of hairs can be lost this way without it being noticeable on the finished fur. Particular attention should be paid to the legs, tail, and head. Their processing is laborious, since they are either very small or require extra work or care because of different skin texture around ears, lips, and the like. As a rule, the scalp and possibly the neck will remain somewhat stiffer than the rest of the fur, which is due to the fact that the skin there is very thick and firm.

In the case of furs that have been removed using the tube method, the legs tend to become unnaturally long and narrow during processing. This can be remedied by inserting the handle of a wooden spoon or other suitable object into the legs from the inside to stretch the skin in this way.

If the hair side of the pelt feels somewhat greasy after tanning is completed

Softening on the beam. In closed spaces, an additional heat source is necessary to advance the drying process.

The tails of animals such as fox, marten, or raccoon require special attention and must also be well greased so that they do not become stiff and brittle. This raccoon tail was tanned so that it lies flat and open.

because some of the tanning solution has seeped into the hair side despite all caution, the hair side can be rubbed with a rag and alcohol. Another method of cleaning and loosening the hair side is to heat a saucepan full of sawdust on the stove and put it in a plastic bag along with the fur.

In it, the fur is well rolled and shaken, and the chips absorb the excess fat. Then remove the fur, shake it out thoroughly, and brush it properly.

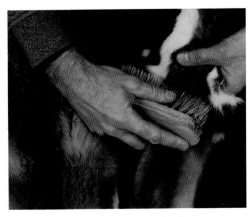

Combing and cleaning pelts with a brush

SMOKING

As previously mentioned in the chapter on tanning pelts, furs do not necessarily have to be smoked either. In addition, sewing together complete furs with head and legs is of course even more time-consuming than pelts and is not really practicable, especially with small animals. However, if you still want to do this, basically proceed as described from p. 98. However, the legs will remain outside the smoker bag and will not get any smoke. As with the skins, of course, only the flesh side is smoked. It is also not advisable to subject the furs to washing after tanning and smoking, since there is no guarantee that the extremities and head area, which had little exposure to the smoke, will automatically remain soft after drying.

A closed tanned fox fur during smoking, hung from the awning with a string. The tail must be kept away from the fire. Here dried sheep dung is being used to generate the smoke.

PROCESSING AND SEWING LEATHER, PELTS, AND FURS

GENERAL

The proud and happy owner of his first successfully tanned leather, pelt, or fur may wonder, after the initial euphoria has subsided somewhat, what to do with it now.

Pelts and furs are in themselves beautiful utilitarian objects and come out wonderfully even without further processing. Lying on the sofa or hanging on the wall, they can be admired, touched, and caressed again and again. But tanning does not mark the end of the flagpole of what is feasible. If you want, the challenge goes further!

It is not for nothing that furriery is traditionally known as an "officially recognized trade." This means that a person has all the knowledge required to perform all the steps from handling the raw material to the finished, usable product. So in the following chapter, you will find some tailoring and sewing projects that should whet your appetite for more. After all, the ultimate goal is, of course, to walk into the office one morning with your self-tanned and self-made moccasins, or to hit the ski slopes wearing your fox fur hat.

Each of the projects presented here can be made from a single finished leather, pelt, or fur. Some projects require relatively little work, such as the "shaman's cap," while others require significantly more effort and dexterity, such as the leather gloves. Therefore, interesting instructions should be found here for both the beginner and the old hand in the field of tailoring.

You should, however, have at least a little experience in needlework and sewing or otherwise calculate more time and patience accordingly. All projects are designed to be sewn by hand. However, almost all leathers, pelts, and furs, except for the thickest layers, can also be sewn with an ordinary household sewing machine and a universal sewing needle. The old craftsman's maxim "Measure twice, cut once" also applies here, because you do not want to unnecessarily ruin a leather or pelt tanned with much diligence and work. Therefore, it is also worthwhile for almost all projects to first make a model of the finished product out of fabric.

The following are descriptions of the tools mentioned in the following part:

Awls: A so-called sewing or pricking awl is needed to punch holes, especially in thick leather or when sewing with leather straps. These awls should have a round tip, not a triangular one with sharp edges, because they are intended only to push the material apart, not cut it.

Needles: Ordinary sewing needles, as used for sewing fabric, are best suited. A 0.03 x 1.6 inches needle should be sufficient for almost all sewing projects. Special leather-sewing needles are not necessary, because these have sharp triangular points that make excessively large holes in the skins.

Thimble: When sewing thick layers, a suitable thimble is necessary to protect the finger from injury. Alternatively, you can wrap the finger with a piece of leather or make a thimble out of leather.

Needlenose Pliers: A small pair of needle-nose pliers with grooved flat jaws that fit comfortably in the hand can be used to guide the needle and can replace a thimble. Their handling requires a little practice, but for sewing thicker layers, they are unbeatable.

Scissors: To cut leather, you need a good, sharp pair of fabric scissors.

Knives: Pelts and furs are not cut with scissors, but with a sharp knife, razor blade, or box knife.

Sewing Thread: Sewing requires thread that is strong and durable. So-called artificial sinew is ideal. It is a synthetic material that can be spliced to a thread of the desired thickness. Instead of sewing or tying a knot at the end of the thread, this material can be melted (with a cigarette lighter) into a tiny ball to prevent slippage. It is necessary to knot the thread at the beginning and the end, or to create small knobs at the beginning and the end of the sewing process with the help of a lighter. Leave about 0.15 to 0.20 inches of the thread standing and melt it up to the workpiece and, if necessary, press it carefully with your fingers. But like a knot, for aesthetic reasons the melted end should be placed on the inside of the workpiece or on a side away from view. Of course, you can also use sturdy cotton or linen yarn.

Leather Straps: These are cut with scissors from your own leather. Watch out for weak areas, knife cuts, and varying thickness of the leather. It is necessary to adjust the cutting width in order to obtain a consistently stable strap. After cutting, the strap must be stretched vigorously, which reduces its flexibility and at the same time tests its tensile strength. One end of the strap is left with a pointed tip about three-quarters of an inch long. This tip is moistened slightly and twisted between the fingers to form a working tip. This allows the strap to be easily pushed through the prepunched holes after drying.

Tape Measure: A flexible tape measure is needed for most work. A 12-inch ruler is also helpful.

Cardboard/Fabric: Thin cardboard is needed for making templates. Occasionally it is also advisable to have a piece of sturdy fabric (e.g., from old jeans) on hand for making test pieces. This allows you to see where adjustments and changes need to be made to the template. This is always better than cutting valuable leather or fur, only to find out afterward that something is too short or too small.

Pins: Occasionally, pins can be useful for joining individual parts as a test before sewing.

Markers: For marking on tanned skin, ballpoint pens and fine felt-tip pens are very effective and leave clearly visible markings; however, these cannot be removed. If you still want to use them, be sure to cut inside the marks, so that they remain on the residual material and not on the workpiece. Otherwise, you can use a soft pencil or special tailor's chalk.

Work Surface: A flat, clean, and, if necessary, cut-resistant surface made of wood or plastic is required.

LEATHER PROJECTS

Working with soft leather, made using the method described here, differs in some respects from the sewing of fabric and from commercially produced leather goods. Each individual hide is different in terms of size, thickness, and possibly the degree of suppleness. The leathers retain their natural variations in terms of thickness. Industrially tanned hides are split or at least evened out (i.e., thinned out in thick areas), which means that they are reduced to a consistent thickness almost throughout, similar to a fabric. Basically, our material is very thin and stretchy on the flanks and often does not lie completely flat. The neck, on the other hand, is generally very thick and firm, but occasionally also coarse grained and loose. An exception is the fallow deer, whose neck area, it turns out, is quite thin. The buttocks at the end of the rump also consist of thicker and firmer material. All these factors must be taken into account when choosing leathers and before cutting.

Compared to fabric, leather has the advantage that the edges do not have to be hemmed to avoid fraying.

On the other hand, such edges can stretch and become wavy over time. Basically, leather behaves a little like stretch fabric, which stretches a bit but eventually wants to return to its original shape. In general, however, leather adapts ideally to the shape of the body after prolonged wear, as in the case of the moccasins shown here. In addition, the fibers of self-tanned leather are very tear resistant, because they have not been weakened by aggressive chemicals, so stitches can be placed very close to the edge.

The leather produced by an average-sized fallow deer is sufficient to make a pair of

Moccasins of the type made by the Native Americans of the eastern woodlands

moccasins as well as a pair of gloves, with sufficient leftovers for other small projects, such as bags, pouches, and thongs.

A selection of awls and a good pair of scissors are indispensable for leatherwork.

MOCCASINS IN THE TRADITIONAL STYLE OF NORTH AMERICAN WOODLAND INDIANS

Such footwear is particularly soft and cuddly, virtually a kind of leather stocking. The moccasins are particularly suitable for wear as slippers, but also for walking in meadows and in the forest. The upper and sole of this footwear are made from a single piece of leather. After completion, another piece of leather can be added as an additional sole to increase durability. Only one template is needed for this type of shoe, because the same shoe is made twice. Only after they have been worn for some time will there be a distinct difference between left and right.

Medium-weight leather is particularly suitable for this purpose.

The Template

You will need a sufficiently large piece of cardboard to create the template.

The steps for this are as follows:

1. On the cardboard, first draw a vertical centerline, the mirror axis. Place one foot on it, with the line running down the middle of the foot, and draw its outline.
2. Now use a tape measure to measure the circumference of the foot at the arch, the thickest part of the foot right at the ankle.
3. Next, determine the center of the foot and mark this point on the mirror axis. From this point, draw a horizontal line

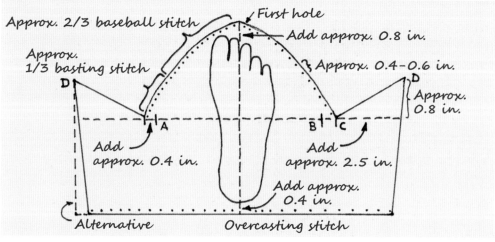

Cutting pattern for woodland Native American moccasins

at right angles to the mirror axis. Mark the circumference of the foot (A–B) in the center of this line and add about 0.4 inches on each side for the seam (point C) and another 2.4 inches for the overhanging sides of the shoe, which will be folded over later.

4. At the heel, also add about 0.4 inches before drawing a line parallel to the A–B line. This is connected at the end at a right angle and thus parallel to the mirror axis with the extended A–B line and goes about three-quarters of an inch beyond it. This results in point D. This line represents the outer edge of the side parts. Now connect points C and D.

5. The last thing to do is to add three-quarters of an inch at the mirror axis above the toes, and from this point draw a curved line toward point C and D.

The exact shape of the arch has to do with the individual foot and cannot be specified exactly. If the arch is too flat, the shoe will be too tight. Therefore, it is advisable to leave a little extra material and possibly make adjustments during sewing. Adjustments must then also be transferred to the template so that it is correct for the second shoe and for all subsequent ones that you may want to make. The template is now ready and is cut out.

Placing the Template and Cutting the Leather

Usually the smoother grain side (hair side) forms the outside of leather products, and the flesh side faces the wearer. Accordingly, the pattern is now placed on the skin and traced there twice. Here one orients oneself ideally at the long centerline of the skin, the backbone. It is important that the template is placed at the same height on the left and right in order to obtain two pieces of leather that are as identical as possible in terms of thickness and elasticity. Because nothing is more uncomfortable than walking around in moccasins, one of which is thick and stiff, and the other thin and baggy.

Sewing

Sewing is done with leather straps, which should each be about 10 inches long. All holes are made with the awl and should be about 0.4 in apart. With thicker leather the distance can be rather greater, and with thin correspondingly less. You can mark the holes beforehand or rely on your visual judgment. Since the leather is very tear resistant, the holes may be placed very close to the edge. If you are unsure, you should first make a few test stitches on a piece of scrap leather. To punch the holes, fold the leather along the mirror axis, place it on the work surface, and perforate both thicknesses at the same time with the awl.

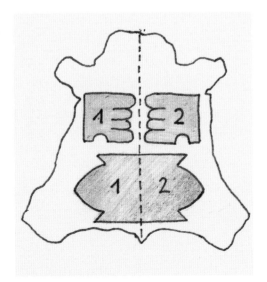

Possible positioning of the templates for moccasins (*bottom*) and gloves

All the seam holes are prepunched with an awl.

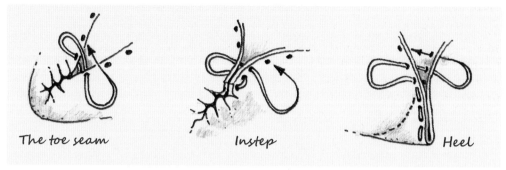

The toe seam *Instep* *Heel*

Diagram for sewing the toe, instep, and heel of the moccasins

However, during sewing it will be necessary to briefly widen the hole again with the awl before passing the strap through. Sewing is started at the toe, with a simple knot at the end of the strap to prevent slipping. Sewing is done from the inside out. That is, if you have pulled the strap from the inside of the leather through the first hole, you now thread it again from the inside/flesh side through the second opposite hole and so on. This results in the typical gathered seam of this shoe. It is important to always tighten the strap; otherwise the gathered seam will remain loose and unsightly.

About two finger widths before the end of the seam at the instep, change the stitching technique and go to a basting stitch to finish the seam. The heel seam is sewn from the bottom up, using a simple

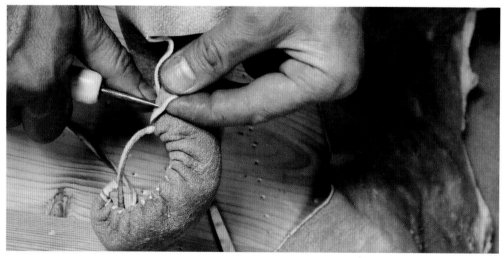

While sewing, occasionally use the awl to widen one of the prepunched holes.

overlock technique. During sewing, you should occasionally try on the shoe and, if necessary, adjust the pattern. The finished moccasins may appear a little tight at the beginning; however, they widen with use and fit the shape of the foot perfectly. Also, while wearing the shoes, a small protruding triangle will form under the heel at the seam. This can be left as it is, or you can turn it inward.

THREE-FINGER GLOVES

The so-called three-finger glove has been known since the Middle Ages. There are various models; for example, with a separate index finger, which also allows the wearer to pull the trigger of a rifle. However, it is always a cross between a fingered glove and a mitten. The model thus offers better thermal insulation than the finger glove and at the same time greater freedom of movement than the mitten.

In the variant depicted here, the index and middle fingers, as well as the ring finger and little finger, are accommodated separately. The gloves can be worn in winter over woolen inner gloves. For this, of course, they must be made accordingly

Two pairs of gloves. The type described here can be seen on the right.

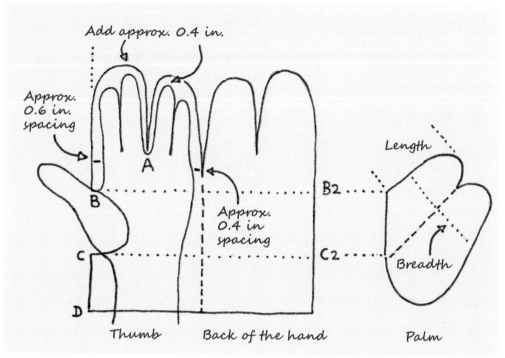

Cutting pattern for the three-finger gloves: main part and separate thumbs

larger. Making gloves to fit accurately is not an easy task, and it is therefore also recommended in this case to experiment with fabric first after completing the template and to apply any resulting changes to the template.

Medium-weight leather is particularly suitable for this purpose.

You will need cardboard, fabric, scissors, needle, sewing thread, thimble/needle-nose pliers, pencil, ruler, tape measure.

The Template for the Main Section

The glove is made of a main section and a separate thumb part. For this purpose, one creates a template for each, which is then used for both the left and the right hand.

The steps for this are as follows:

1. Place one hand (in the case of the drawing, the right one) on the cardboard so that the thumb is spread and the two pairs of fingers are also slightly spread. Draw the outline of the hand with the pencil. Now mark points A, B, and C. Point A is exactly where the middle and ring fingers meet at the palm. B is in the

bend between the thumb and index finger, and C is at the point where the base of the thumb meets the wrist.

2. Note that the basic shape of the template is an elongated rectangle. The parallel sides should be about 0.6 inches apart to the right and left of the hand. The arcs for the fingers are now drawn in freehand. They meet at point A and should be spaced about 0.4 inches apart at the fingertips. The total length of the glove, and thus the distance from B to C, is up to you. However, it should be at least 1.6 to 2 inches. Significantly longer lengths of 4 to 4.75 inches provide the opportunity to fold the ends of the gloves cuff-like.

3. The recess for the thumb is also drawn freehand and is similar to a bulbous, hanging D.

4. Now cut out the model of the palm up to the dotted line, fold it over at this line, and trace the outline, except for the recess for the thumb.

The Template for the Thumbs

1. The separate template for the thumb is created by first transferring the distance between points B and C onto it.

2. Measure the length of the thumb from point B to above the tip with the tape measure. Then measure the circumference by placing the tape measure loosely around the thickest part of the thumb. Now enter both lengths. Both lengths must be measured generously to leave room for the seam and a possible inner glove.

3. The curvatures for the base of the thumb and the thumb tip are drawn in freehand.

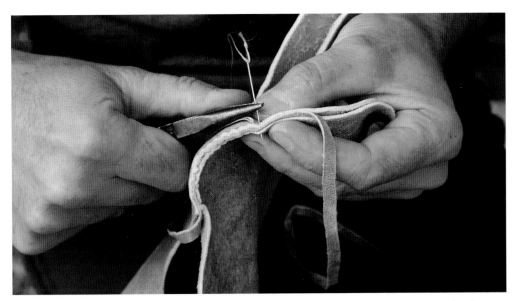

Sewing the gloves with a pair of needlenose pliers. The needle is not held with the fingers but is pushed through the leather with the help of pliers.

Placing the Templates and Cutting the Leather

Here, too, the templates should be placed on the skin in such a way as to ensure that all parts are made of leather of comparable thickness. Also in this case, one uses the imaginary back line of the leather as orientation. In addition, after marking for the first glove, do not forget to position the template as a mirror image for the second, so as not to accidentally get two right or two left gloves.

Sewing

The gloves are usually sewn from the outside, using a basting stitch. However, if the seam is to be inside and out of sight, it must be made accordingly larger, and the glove is turned inside out after completion. The seam can be placed very close, about 0.04 in from the edge of the leather. It is recommended that a reinforcing strip be sewn into the seam as well. This is a strip of leather about 0.20 inches wide, which stabilizes and emphasizes the seam. This should be of medium thickness and of course sufficiently long. Small stitches and conscientious sewing are not essential for functionality, but neat, even sewing increases the value of the work and earns praise and recognition. As you sew, keep trying on the glove and adjusting the cut as necessary. Since the needle must be passed through three layers, one will have to wear a thimble or else use a pair of grooved needlenose pliers to guide the needle. Right-handed people usually sew from right to left, with the left hand holding the halves to be sewn together tightly along with the reinforcing strips, and the right hand guiding the needle.

FUR PROJECTS

A finished tanned fur is beautiful in itself and can easily be used as a throw for sofas and armchairs, as a base in a stroller, or as a blanket, bedspread, rug, or wall hanging. The same is true for many furs.

But of course, since time immemorial, skins and furs have been processed around the globe into a wide variety of utility and clothing items, especially where climatic conditions made warm clothing necessary. The rich cultural legacies in this area are proof of the great craftsmanship and artistic skill of the various peoples when it comes to ideally combining functionality and aesthetics. Pelts and furs of different animals vary considerably in terms of the characteristics of the skin and the quality, color, and texture of the hair—and not only in terms of age and sex and the time of slaughter, but also within the same fur. Making the most of these natural differences and nuances is a fine art and represents both the attraction and the challenge of working with these materials.

The patterns provided here are intended to serve as a basic framework, which may require certain adjustments when transferred to the fur of another animal species. When transferring the templates to the pelt or even to the fur of an animal, some things must be taken into account. First, as with

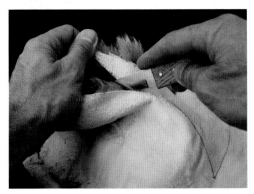

Pelts and furs are cut from the flesh side with a knife, in order to avoid damaging the hairs.

this would cut off not only the skin, but precisely the hair, and mostly in an uncontrollable and unsightly way. Therefore, it is necessary to cut skins and furs from the flesh side, using a knife. The knife should be very sharp. Razor blades are also very suitable for this purpose. For cutting, the fur can be placed on a solid base. However, care must be taken not to cut with too much pressure, so as not to pinch the hair between the blade and the pad and cut it off as well. It is therefore necessary only to cut or score the hide and leave the coat undamaged.

leather, the skin has different thicknesses and stretch in different places. But the biggest difference from leather is the presence of the natural hair coat. When placing the template on the flesh side of a pelt or fur, it is therefore important to pay attention to the length and coloring, and especially the flow of the hair. In all animals, the hair basically runs from the back of the head over the shoulders toward the tail. On the legs, it is oriented from the center of the body downward, toward the hooves or paws. With wool-bearing animals, such as sheep or bison, detecting a flow is almost impossible. In the shoulder area there is often a vertebra, which directs the hair radially in all directions. Occasionally there are also swirls on the belly or in the flank area, whereas under the legs, the armpits, the hair is often very sparse or not present at all. These gradients vary in different species and should be closely examined before placing the template.

Trimming furs and pelts also requires a different approach than leather, which is again due to the hair. It can be cut with scissors only in the rarest cases, since

Another option is to cut the fur or pelt freehand. The means, for example, to fix it on the floor with a foot or knee, stretch it tightly with one hand, and then guide the blade with the other. If you do not have the confidence to make a proper cut along the marked line in this way, you should first practice a little on leftover pieces.

Furs and skins are usually sewn from the flesh side. This is done with a normal household sewing needle. When sewing very thin furs, you do not need a thimble or needlenose pliers for needle guidance. With thicker material, however, this is necessary to protect the fingers from injury. Furs and pelts are often not as tear resistant as leather. This means that the seams should be a little farther away from the edge of the cut, and the thread pulled less tightly. Here, too, you should carry out several test stitches on remnants to get a clear picture of the stability of the fur being used. Sewing is always done from right to left, while for left-handers it is in the other direction. This means that the needle is

The finished cap made of fur
from a fallow deer, in this case
with the seam in the front

guided with the right hand while the left holds the workpiece together at the seam. As the sewing progresses, it is occasionally necessary to move the hairs that slip into the seam outward or downward with the fingers. It is important not to sew any hair into the seam, which would result in an unsightly, shaggy, and bulging seam. For this reason, it is also advisable, if possible, to always sew with the natural flow of the hair and not against it, because especially with unruly or coarse hair, stroking it out of the seam is otherwise very difficult.

THE ICEMAN CAP

In 1992, the Neolithic glacier mummy "Ötzi" was found in the Alps. This man was completely dressed in fur and leather and therefore represents a rich resource in terms of the use of skins as well as sewing techniques and patterns during this era. Part of the iceman's equipment was a perfectly preserved cap made of bearskin. The rudimentary pattern has been preserved in detail and can be reproduced in any way. Of course, fur from deer, sheep, or any other animal can be used as the starting material. A variation of the original pattern is presented here to reduce the amount of sewing.

The Templates

The cap consists of two parts: the main section and the top piece or crown. Separate templates are made for these. All measurements are intended for adults.

1. The main part is made from a single piece. This is an elongated rectangular strip, the length of which corresponds to the circumference of the head, measured at forehead level above the eyebrows, length A–B. In the original bear skin there were two strips, which were sewn together parallel to one another. The height of the strip is approximately obtained by dividing the length by a factor of 4.5. That is, with a head circumference at 23 inches, you get a height of

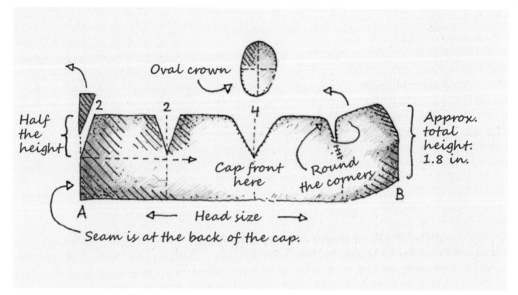

Cutting pattern for the "Ötzi" cap

5 inches.

2. Now transfer these measurements to the cardboard for the template. Determine half the height, mark it on the cardboard, and draw a line at this height from one end of the strip to the other.

3. Then divide the entire length of the strip by four and enter these measurements. This also gives the center of the template, which will later be the front of the cap.

4. Now, it's necessary to take a wedge from the top of the template at each of the four marked divisions. This is necessary to reduce the top diameter of the cap so that it will later fit the curvature of the head. The wedge at the front should be about 4 fingers wide, or about 2.4 inches, and the wedges at the sides and back of the head about 2 fingers wide, or 1.2 inches. Since the ends of the main strip will eventually be sewn together and form the back of the cap, the wedge is only half the size of the others.

5. All the resulting corners can be slightly rounded.

The template for the cap crown is made only after sewing together the main part.

To do this, first make an appropriately sized symmetrical oval by eye. This is then inserted into the hat from the inside to the upper opening. By marking with a pencil, you can now directly determine the exact size and cut the template accordingly.

Position the Templates and Cut the Fur

When transferring the template to the pelt, it is important to remember that caps are generally designed so that the hair falls down. However, a sideways sweep is also conceivable A part of the fur with a swirl is particularly suitable for the cap crown.

The hair flow of a deerskin

When working with pelts and furs, always pay attention to the direction of flow of the hair.

Basically, you should consider achieving as even a finish as possible, as far as the hair flow is concerned, so that a natural impression is created from the outside and no seams are visible.

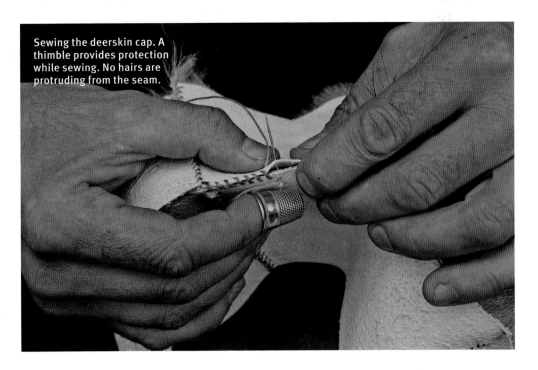

Sewing the deerskin cap. A thimble provides protection while sewing. No hairs are protruding from the seam.

Sewing

Again, experimenting on remnants beforehand is recommended. For the entire cap,
as in the original, use the overlock stitch.
Of course, an even and fine seam is much
more attractive than a roughly executed
one, even if it is not visible from the outside when the cap is worn.

Once the hat is sewn, the hair can be left
natural at the bottom edge or trimmed with
scissors to form a clear, straight line. If you
wish, you can finish the cap with a fabric
lining.

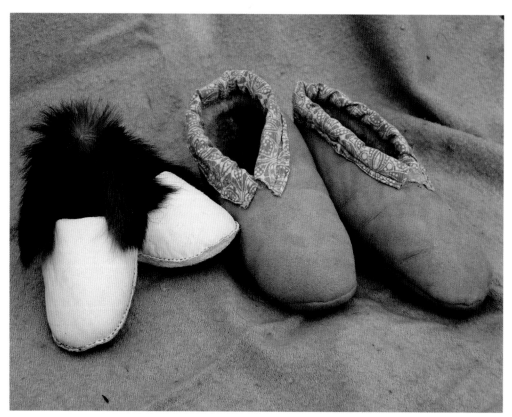

Two pairs of fur slippers. Those on the left are deerskin, sewn from the outside, while those on the
right are lambskin, sewn from the inside.

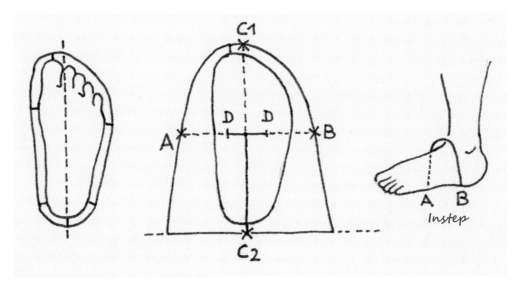

A basic cutting pattern for fur shoes.

KAMIKS AND MUKLUKS

A variety of different patterns for fur boots and the corresponding inner shoes have been handed down by the circumpolar peoples, such as the Inuit. These were mainly made from seal and caribou skins. Variations of these traditional styles can be made from sheepskin, lambskin, or the winter fur of deer, for example. They make warm slippers or cottage shoes because the fur is worn inside as a warming insulation.

The model shown here is a simple cut, which basically consists of two separate parts, but can be supplemented with an extended shaft. This can also be made of fur, or fabric or felt.

The Templates

1. For the sole template, place a foot on a piece of cardboard and trace around it. To this basic shape, add some space all around. How much you add to the sides depends very much on the fur you use, or on the length and density of the hair coat. With the hair, it's like wearing two or three pairs of extra socks in your shoes, and they have to be correspondingly larger. The flatter the hair lies, the less addition is necessary and the more the template can follow the anatomical contour of the foot, so one will make a right and a left shoe. In the case of very thick coats, such as some unshorn sheepskins or the dense winter coat of deer, which can easily reach a length of 1.6 inches, the sole will tend to take the shape of a regular oval, and one will no longer distinguish between left and right. In order to estimate approximately how much allowance is necessary, place the foot on the part of the fur from which

the sole is to be cut. Now, as a test, fold the fur slightly upward all around, approximately to the upper edge of the toes. As a rough average value, an addition of the width of a little finger can be assumed. Basically, it makes sense to always add a little more, because if you have to make adjustments while sewing, it is annoying to realize that you were too frugal and therefore an entire part has to be replaced.

2. The additional width is then used to draw a second line around the outline of the foot. This does not exactly follow every anatomical curve and turn of the foot but, rather, represents a generalized outline. Then draw the centerline of this outline from the center of the heel to where the big toe meets its nearest neighbor. Now cut out the template.

3. For the upper part template, place the sole template on another, larger piece of cardboard and draw it there. The centerline is also entered here. From it, the center is now determined and a cross line is drawn there at right angles. The instep is transferred to this.

4. The length of the instep is measured directly at the ankle, where the foot joins the leg. Here, too, length variations of an inch or more can occur, depending on the density of the hair coat. The determined length is entered in the center of the transverse line (line A–B).

5. Then it is necessary to add material for the upper leather at the heel and toe as well. Here, too, the width of a finger serves as an approximate guide or as the value already added to the sole (points C1 and C2). At the heel, point C2, running parallel to the transverse line, results in the base line, which finally represents the heel seam.

6. Now, starting from point C1 and crossing points A and B, draw a balanced curved line freehand, which ends on the base line. Finally, determine the points D. They should be about 1.2 to 1.6 inches from the center. Along the line between them and from the center point down to C2, the top will later be cut open to give the opening for the foot.

Placing the Templates on the Pelt

For the sole part, of course, the most suitable parts of the pelt are those where the skin is thick and firm, because here the load and abrasion are greatest. The direction of flow of the coat, if it plays a role, should be oriented toward the toes for both parts; otherwise it will be difficult to slip into the shoes.

It is best to cut out the parts for one shoe first and start sewing it. If changes need to be made, transfer them to the template first before cutting the parts for the second shoe.

Sewing

Since the accuracy of fit could only be approximated with the templates, the sole and upper are stitched together at five or six points each with a stitch or pins, leaving the heel part open. From there, one carefully slips into the provisional arrangement. In this way, it soon becomes clear where adjustments need to be made. Once you're sure the shoe will fit, you start sewing at the top of the foot, about where point C1 is, and follow one side all the way to the heel. Then you start at the top again and sew along the other side until the seams meet at the heel and the entire sole is joined to the upper. Occasionally the two sides do not meet exactly and there is an overhang. This is removed until the two sides are an exact fit again. Then you sew the heel seam closed. Sew with the basting stitch from the flesh side. The use of the overlock stitch is not suitable, because the abrasion during walking endangers the seams.

It's advisable not to cut off unruly hairs and hairs protruding from the seam, which can be the case especially on the toes and on skins with a pronounced hairline, before sewing, but to brush them inward as before.

However, it is also possible to sew from the fur side. However, this is recommended only for short-haired or shorn skins. In this case, the shoe is sewn upside down and turned inside out at the end through the foot opening. The seam is then hidden and is protected, especially when walking.

PELT PROJECTS

SHAMAN'S CAP

This particular headgear is made from a single complete and barely cut fox fur. It is therefore particularly suitable for the proud tanner who wants to use his fur after the work is done, but wants to preserve it in its integrity. This model makes a sensational piece of headgear, with the main part of the fur, as well as the hind legs and tail, falling freely down the wearer's back. At the same time, as long as the fur is large enough, the hood provides additional protection for the neck and throat in windy and cold conditions when the back portion is brought forward and wrapped around the neck.

Construction

Making a template in this case is of no use because each fur is different in size and texture. In addition, this headdress is not a tailor-made furrier work, but rather a loose-fitting headgear, which is held in place by a chin strap. Therefore, it is important to mark the cutting lines only on the pattern drawing and to proceed with a sense of proportion. However, you should not rely blindly on the drawings shown here, but should first pin the pieces together and then check their appearance and accuracy of fit in front of the mirror.

The finished
cap

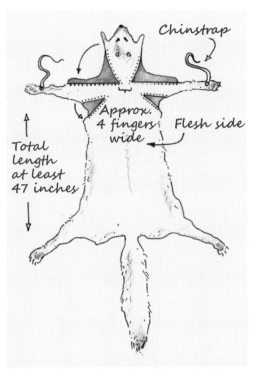

Chinstrap

Approx.
4 fingers
wide

Flesh side

Total
length
at least
47 inches

Cutting pattern for the shaman's cap. The four dark-shaded areas are removed, after which the edges are sewn together.

In this hood, the head fur and a piece of the animal's forearms are sewn to its front legs by means of four separate stitches to create a cavity for the animal's own head. As for the initial shape of the fur to be processed, it is desirable that the skin of the lower jaw on both sides of the head is also preserved and reasonably softly

tanned, because a piece of the foreleg is sewn to it. If this is not the case, the legs can also be sewn directly to the side of the head. However, this reduces the opening for one's own head somewhat. Depending on how the cut was made during skinning, the small wedge-shaped cutouts below the front legs must also be placed a little farther up. Therefore, wedges 1 and 2 below the head are also removed first and the seams are executed, and only then wedges 3 and 4, in order to be able to make appropriate adjustments.

Last, a leather strap about 0.2 inches wide is sewn on the end of each front leg, just above the paw. These can be tied together under the chin, keeping the hood in place.

Sewing

Many of the peculiarities of sewing pelts have already been mentioned in the chapter on sewing fur, so they will not be repeated here. It will be noted that the skin of the head fur of a fox is quite thick and stiff, while that on the forearms, on the other hand, is very thin and delicate. Accordingly, care must be taken when sewing. Here, too, sewing is done from the flesh side, either with the overlock or the baseball stitch.

The trapper's cap with, in this case, the front paws as ear flaps.

TRAPPER'S CAP

I was introduced to this classic cap model in the 1990s by trapper and tanner George Michaud in the USA. This winter cap can be made from a single large fox fur. Alternatively, one can of course use several smaller skins from other animals, such as hare or nutria, for example. Although the cap is made of several individual parts, it should appear from the outside as if made of one piece. This is achieved by the overlapping hair coat flow, which should hide all the seams.

The Templates

The measurements provided are for a head circumference of 23 inches. If the circumference differs, the dimensions must be adjusted accordingly. All cardboard parts are produced and cut out according to the specifications.

Placing the Templates and Cutting Out the Pieces

When placing the templates on the flesh side of the skin, one must play with the individual parts a little to find the ideal positioning. In doing so, pay attention to the thickness and possibly the waviness of the skin, and the quality and color gradient of the hair on the side of the pelt. The flow of the hair on the finished cap should run from the forehead to the back of the neck. Middle strips and side pieces give the cap its basic shape. Ear flaps and neck piece are optional. Also, their placement on the pelt can vary, as shown. For example, you can keep the tail to cover the neck or use the legs as ear flaps, as in the photo.

Once you have decided, cut out the main parts and sew them together before starting on the rest.

Sewing

Sewing is done from the flesh side, using the overlock stitch. For this purpose, points A on the side parts are pinned to points B on the center strip by sewing them with a single stitch. It is important to pay attention to the hair flow of the side parts, which should run from the face to the back. The same also applied to the middle part. From these center points, now sew downward in an arc, respectively from the right and left. In the process, you will notice

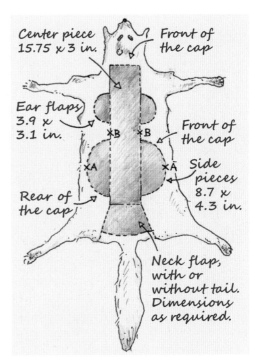

Center piece 15.75 x 3 in.

Front of the cap

Ear flaps 3.9 x 3.1 in.

×B   ×B

Front of the cap

×A   ×A

Side pieces 8.7 x 4.3 in.

Rear of the cap

Neck flap, with or without tail. Dimensions as required.

Positioning of the templates on the fox pelt

that the fur parts may stretch a little and do not want to end exactly with the end of the middle strip. You have to pay attention to this during sewing, so that there is not too much material left over when finished or the cap does not become symmetrical. If you would like the cap to have neck protection and earflaps, these are also attached beforehand with a basting stitch and sewn on in the same way. Done!

If you want, you can add a fabric lining to this cap. For this purpose, any thin and soft fabric is suitable. To make it, cut out all of the individual parts of the cap once again with the help of the templates; each time you need to allow for an allowance of about half a centimeter for folding the hem.

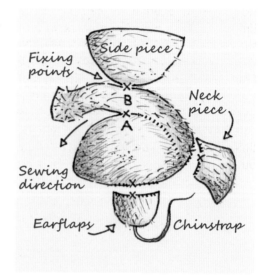

Assembling the various fur parts of the trapper's cap

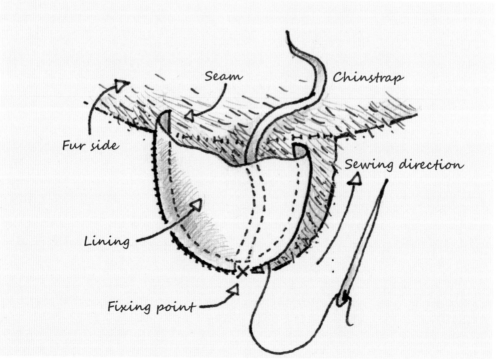

Installing an inner lining, using the earflaps as an example

Now first sew together the main part of the lining. Then you put this right side in over the hair side of the finished cap and fix it in a few places with pins. Now sew the lining on all around, except at the back of the head, where an area of about 4 inches is left open. Through this slit, you now carefully turn the cap inside out so that the lining is on the inside and the fur is on the outside again. Then close the remaining opening. If the neck guard and ear flaps are also present, they now receive their lining in the same way, and the open areas of the individual lining parts are sewn to the lining of the main part at the very end.

If a chin strap is desired, it can be sewn right along with the lining inside the ear flaps and then come out when you turn it around.

FURTHER READING

- Anders, Jess, *Book on Painting Hides —a Plains Indian Tradition*, Amazon, Martson Gate 2012.
- Baillargeon, Morgan, *North American Aboriginal Hide Tanning*, Mercury Series, Canadian Museum of Civilization, 2010.
- Belitz, Larry, *Brain Tanning the Sioux Way*, Pine Ridge Indian Reservation, 1973.
- Doganalp-Votzi, Heidemarie, *Der Gerber, der Kulturbringer*, European University Publications, Peter Lang Verlag, 1997.
- Edholm, Steven, and Tamara Wilder, Wet-Scrape Braintanned Buckskin, Paleotechnics, Boonville, CA, 1997.
- Ewers, John C., *Blackfeet Crafts*, R. Schneider, 1986.
- Fleckinger, Angelika, and Hubert Steiner, *Der Mann aus dem Eis*, South Tyrol Museum of Archaeology, 1998.
- Gansser, A., "Principles of Tanning," *Ciba Review* 81 (1950).
- Grant, Bruce, *Leather Braiding*, Cornell Maritime, Atglen, PA, 1978.
- Gross, Günter, *Und wie war das früher —Von einem der ältesten Gewerbe und des Leders Werdegang*, Dippoldiswalde District Museum, 1991.
- Hiller, Wesley, "Hidatsa Soft Tanning of Hides," *Minnesota Archaeologist*, January 1948.
- Holfeld, Monika, *Fischleder gerben: Von Fischhaut zu Fischleder*, self-published, Berlevag, Norway, 2018.
- Kitzmann, Matthias, "Felle von Dachs, Fuchs, Waschbär, selber gemacht," *Traditional Archery* 39 (2006).
- Klek, Markus, *American Indian Buffalo Robes: A Study of their Role in Native Societies and a Practical Guide to Traditional Tanning Techniques*, BoD Norderstedt, 2008.
- Klek, Markus, *Ahle versus Nadel: Experimente zum Nähen von Fell und Leder während der Urzeit*, EXAR Bilanz, Unteruhldingen, 2012.
- Klek, Markus, *Auf der Suchen ach dem Naβschaber—Archäologie und funktionale Analyse von Gerbewerkzeug aus Knochen mit längsstehender Arbeitskante*, EXAR Bilanz, Oldenburg, 2011.
- Klokkernes, Torunn, "Skin Processing Technology in Eurasian Reindeer Cultures," PhD diss., Museum of Cultural History, Oslo, 2007.

- Lehmann, Paulus, *Gesundes Wohnen— Gesunde Kleidung*, Institute for Building Biology, Neubeuren, 1984.
- Lorenz, Friedrich, *Rauchwarenkunde*, Volk und Wissen Verlag, Berlin and Leipzig, 1951.
- Lyford, Carrie, *Quill and Beadwork of the Western Sioux*, R. Schneider, 1983.
- Mason, Otis, *Aboriginal Skin Dressing*, Annual Report of the US National Museum, 1889.
- Mauch, Heiko, "Studien zur Lederherstellung am Beispiel des nördlichen Alpenraums," Dissertation, University of Tübingen, 2004.
- McPherson, John, *Indianische Hirngerbung*, Hudsons Bay Indian Trading Post, 2005.
- Michaud, George, "Fur Brain Tanning," *Bulletin of Primitive Technology* 21 (2001).
- Miller, Jim, *Brain Tan Buffalo Robes, Skins and Pelts*, Sundborn, St. Clair, MI, 1997.
- Moog, Gerhard Ernst, *Der Gerber: Professionelle Lederherstellung*, Verlag Eugen Ulmer, 2016.
- Oakes, Jill, *Die Kunst der Inuit Frauen— Stolze Stiefel, Schätze aus Fell*, Frederking & Thaler, Munich, 1996.
- Ottinger, Helmut, and Ursula Reeb, *Gerben*, Ulmer Verlag, Stuttgart, 2013.
- Peter, Katherine, *How I Tan Hides*, Alaska Native Language Center, 1980.
- Pfeiffer, Dominique, *Gerben mit natürlichen und chemischen Stoffen*, BoD Norderstedt, 2010.
- Rahme, Lotta, *Leather*, Carber Press, 1995.
- Reichert, Anne, "Rekonstruktion der Ötzi Schuhe," *Experimental Archaeology*, Summary 1998, Supplement 24, Isensee Verlag, 1999.
- Richards, Matt, "Brains, Bones and Hot Springs: Native American Deerskin Dressing at the Time of Contact," *Bulletin of Primitive Technology* 12, 1996.
- Scheer, A., *Von der Rohhaut bis zur Kleidung*, Ice Age Workshop, Museum Booklet 2, Prehistoric Museum Blaubeuren, 1995.
- Society of Friends of the Tanning Museum, *Die Lohmühle von Leustettin*, Leustettin, 2013.
- Terpack, Vaughn, "Observations on Goatskin," *Bulletin of Primitive Technology* 16.
- Thijsse, Saskia, "Die Herstellung einer Frauentracht an Hand von Grabungsfunden der Swifterbant-Kultur," *Experimental Archaeology*, Summary 1998, Supplement 24, Isensee Verlag, 1999.
- Torrence, Gaylord, *The American Indian Parfleche*, University of Washington Press, 1994.
- Wiener, Ferdinand, *Die Weißgerberei*, A. Hartlebens Verlag, 1904.
- Wilder, Edna, *Secrets of Eskimo Skin Sewing*, Alaska North West, Anchorage, 1976.
- Wood, Guy, "Basic Footwear of the Southeastern Tribes," *Bulletin of Primitive Technology* (Spring 2000).

Markus Klek lived in the US for nine years, and while there, he was introduced to the ancient art of tanning by Native Americans. He runs his own small tannery and makes leather clothing. He passes on his knowledge by teaching popular tanning courses. He lives in Schramberg, Germany. See his work and courses at https://www.markusklek.de.